P9-DGD-552

Dear Lovers—

Here is an unfinished book.
It is yet to be completed
by you. More important than
what I have written will be
what *you* write! Please take
the time—and love—to jot
beside the opening photos
your own private, special
moments. And as you read the
book, answer the questions
and talk about them with
each other. The purpose of
the book is to bring you
closer together. That's the
best thing you can do to
make your marriage great!

Happy writing (and reading)

Enjoy,

Chuck

Fr. Chuck Gallagher

Library of Congress Catalog
Card Number: 77-80818

Published by William H. Sadlier, Inc.,
New York, Chicago, Los Angeles and
Serendipity House, Box 461, Scottdale,
Pennsylvania 15683. Printed in U.S.A.

© 1977 Chuck Gallagher. All rights reserved.

ISBN: 0-8215-6467-6
123456789/987

Home Office: 11 Park Place, New York, N.Y. 10007

HURRAH FOR PARENTS!

by Fr. Chuck Gallagher, S.J.

edited and arranged by Bob and Lois Blewett

Worldwide Marriage Encounter

William H. Sadlier, Inc.

NEW YORK • CHICAGO • LOS ANGELES

Small things, big things,
make up TODAY —
the greatest day of our lives!

Discovering
our love
all over
again.

Two sisters giggling.

Getting together with Grandpa about a fishing trip.

Treasuring long-lost Stars

A skinned knee, healing.

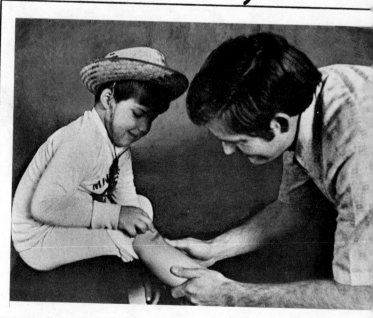

A doll for the birthday princess.

A time for being down.

A time for being up.

Family portrait time —
and boundless energy.

Expectations can
be an inspiration
To your child,
open horizons,
encourage him.

1

EXPECTATIONS

What is the difference between expectations and dreams?

Your answer:

Expectations are those things that we are quite certain will take place. We are certain to the point of making preparations. Our expectations can be good or bad. We expect our children to go to school, so we acquaint them with color crayons, teach them to tie their shoes and repeat their addresses. We expect our children to sometimes fall and scrape their knees at the playground, so we urge them to be careful. Dreams are things that don't have much certainty, but we may want them very much and may work hard to attain them. They may become expectations. When our dreams are negative, they are nightmares.

What dreams do you have for your children?

Your answer:

Even before a man and woman marry they usually dream about the children they may have one day. After marriage, during pregnancies and afterwards as the children grow, their dreams increase. One of the most endearing qualities of parents is how much thought they give their children before they are born and during their years of childhood.

Their dreams likely center on the types of personalities and talents their sons and daughters will have as well as on how they will look—as children. In early adulthood we seldom, if at all, think of our future children as adults. We think about them as babies. It's only after they're born—or are in school—that we begin to think about what they'll be like when they grow up. It's then that we consider what kind of marriage partners they will be, whom they'll marry, what kind of jobs they'll have, how much income, the type of persons they'll be with others. We might even dream about how we'll enjoy them in later years, how good it will be to have an adult relationship with them, to be able to really talk things over with them.

High on our priority list for them is a happy life. We care about their well-being. And it's part of our ambition to smooth the way for them, making sure that they will have a better life as adults than we have had. We know that they have to learn to stand on their own two feet. We look on the present as a time for preparation. Our gift to them is to make sure they're ready for adult life—able to cope with it.

Each of us has different dreams for our children. So right now is a good time to sit back and bring to mind exactly how we see our children now and in the future, filling in all the details. We don't often take time to put it all together, to look at the whole picture. So, let's dream along and bring to the surface exactly what's in our hearts for our kids.

counse
ur son
ald be
sident,
ut...

What nightmares do you have about your children?

Your answer:

We have dreams and we have nightmares. Real fears sometimes put a fist on our hearts. It isn't that we don't trust our children or don't believe in their goodness. It's just that we are concerned that the pressures or the circumstances of today's world will hurt them.

We worry about their physical well-being. We worry about drugs and alcohol. We worry about cars. Most of all we worry about our children's lives as persons. Part of our worry comes from knowing that in a number of years we'll have no control over the situations they are in. We want to do enough now to prepare them to deal with the difficulties they may face.

We wonder how they'll turn out. Whether or not they'll get a decent job and be able to support a family. Whether or not she will be a good wife. Will her husband be good to her? Will he be a good husband? Will his wife love him? There is an ache in our hearts about the possible hurts they might have. Who's going to take care of them? Will they be lonely? Oh, we don't want them to be lonely!

We wonder if they're going to accept our personal, moral and religious values or throw them aside. It's a rare parent who hasn't lost sleep thinking about his children's future.

Maybe we don't bring our fears to the surface often. And when they come to mind, we try to push them aside, but they're there, swirling beneath the surface. There are times when we look at our children sleeping or hold their pictures in our hands and wonder. Will he always be a sweet, loving boy? Will she remain a gentle, sensitive girl?

We need to take time now to identify our nightmares, the specific fears that we have for our children. We need to zero in on them.

Do your dreams come from your hopes for yourself?

Your answer:

We love our children and want the best for them. But, unfortunately, what we often think of as best for them turns out to be what is really best for us. We're not being deliberately selfish, but uppermost in our minds are our dreams! We wanted to have a college education or be a doctor or live in a particular type house. We wish we had married a certain kind of person or had a lot of friends. These things are so important to our happiness that we assume they will be just as important to our children. We are seldom as objective as we think we are. The dreams we had—some fulfilled, some unfulfilled—become the dreams we have for our children.

We tend to be less realistic about dreams for our children than we were about dreams for ourselves. When we were directly involved, we were aware of the price of living up to our ambitions, and we recognized our limitations.

Looking back we are rather fuzzy about reality and think that external circumstances or lack of opportunity prevented us from living out our dreams. Consequently, we may think that if we provide the opportunity and our ambition, our children can achieve those dreams.

A lot of times, too, our dreams for our children come from what we consider to have been childhood deprivations. We don't want our children to have to make the sacrifices we or our parents had to make.

Do your dreams come from the hopes of your spouse?

Your answer:

From the beginning of a couple's relationship each takes notice of what is dear to the heart of the other. Because of our love, we have a tendency to take on each other's dreams for our children. We may trade off. That is, I adopt the dreams of my spouse for certain of our children and mine for the others.

But do we truly know the dreams of our spouse? Maybe we don't. We may have adopted them by osmosis. Maybe we never discuss our ambitions—other than what kind of car we'd like some day. It's important for us to know what each other's ambitions are for ourselves and for our children. If we don't know, we can be at cross purposes with each other without even recognizing it. We need to pinpoint each other's dreams. We need to look at them and see how much they have influenced the dreams we have for our children.

Do your nightmares come from your failings?

Your answer:

Most of us are conscious of our defects and deficiencies. We recognize the part they've played in our failure to live up to our hopes. A father who is aware of his laziness, his inconsistency, his inability to get along with others, his lack of education, his dependency on his parents or his harsh relationship with his family is troubled. His nightmares are rooted in this recognition. He doesn't want the children to repeat his mistakes, and yet he is afraid they will.

We're conscious of what we're missing in life, what we want, what we don't have and don't seem able to get. We want to make sure that our children don't go through the same thing. We see how our defects have affected us and we're apprehensive. Those same defects may cause our children to fall into even worse traps! That's where the nightmares come from. From the sense of our own weakness, our self-rejection and unjustifiable guilt.

Most parents have some nightmares during pregnancy as they look forward to the baby's coming. They think about the possibility of the child being born with some defect. They lose sleep over it. The same thing is true as parents look ahead to the child's adulthood. There's the unformulated thought that we don't deserve perfection, that things could turn out badly for us.

Do your nightmares come from the failings of your spouse?

Your answer:

We may see clearly something that has held our spouse back. Maybe he doesn't have the education to get a good job, or he drinks too much, or he just seems to be wasting his life. We're afraid that these failings will be bred into our children or breathed into them by their living with us.

Our attitude toward our spouse can be very compassionate—we see the pain those shortcomings have caused him. And we're frightened that this same hurting experience will come to the children. We may see that he is afraid that it will too. We share his worry and concern. Sometimes his nightmare envelops us more than our own.

Do your dreams and nightmares affect the way you deal with your children?
Your answer:

The goals that we have for our children and the pitfalls that we seek to keep from their experience determine our conduct. Anytime we see an inclination in any of our kids towards taking on one of our defects or slacking off from advancing toward our dream for them, we tend to pressure them. We worry that their marks might not be good enough to get them into college. We're concerned about their hypersensitivity, volatility, laziness, carelessness. We feel that unless we step in immediately and correct it, it may have a serious impact on their future life. We treat our children like little adults! We expect them to have, now, all the virtues and good qualities we want them to have as grown ups— and none of our failings! We are dealing with future possibilities rather than with a present child. We're making plans for him and we're trying to figure out ways to advance those plans. What happens is that we try to fit him into a blueprint, rather than letting him grow at his own pace.

There's no evil or bad will involved. We do have to think ahead for our kids, no one is denying that. We have to correct mistakes and we have to encourage good qualities. The problem comes when we're so filled with thoughts of the child's future life that we lose sight of his present one. Doing that, we fail to experience our child as he is right now. No one really wants to miss out on today, so it's well to be aware of how much we're letting our hopes and fears for the future color our attitudes and decisions.

Today
is the
greatest
day of
our
lives!

21

**What types of
expectations
do you have for
your children?**

Your answer:

Parents' expectations can be general. For example, that their
children grow up to be good and to be happy. Or, they can be
specific. That—in our family of a doctor—our son or daughter
become a doctor. Expectations can be long-term. That each child
find a good spouse or have a substantial bank account. Expectations can be immediate. That my daughter get promoted from
third grade. They can be significant. That the kids keep their faith
in God. Or they can be relatively insignificant—that my son learn
his table manners.

They can be spelled out or hidden, but we have them.

And if we are asked what we want for our children, we would
say, "We want to leave them free. We want them to be themselves, to grow up to be their own man or woman." But the truth
of the matter is, all of us have some definite expectations for our
kids. They may not be the traditional ones. They may not be
easily recognizable. They may not be the ones that other people
have. They may leave the children a lot of freedom and plenty of
room for growth. But we do have them.

When I was a schoolteacher, during July and August I was like
an expectant father. I looked forward to September and dreamed
of what my kids would be like. I was eager for the list of their
names so I could memorize them. I would imagine what each one
might look like. "O'Reilly." He just had to have freckles.
"Schultz." He would be hefty. "Garibaldi." Small and olive-
complexioned. Of course, it turned out that Garibaldi had the
freckles, Schultz was small and swarthy—I forgot about the other
side of the family—and O'Reilly had pimples. Isn't it funny, I
never thought about any of my kids having acne!

Those dreams were very good for me. They helped make my
kids real until the time I could see them with my own eyes, hear
their voices, experience their triumphs and failures, joys and sor-

rows. This anticipation brought them alive to me until fall. Then I could sit on top of my desk and scoop them all up into my heart with my eyes, ride on the bus and sing all sorts of crazy songs with them, cheer at their games, wrestle with them in the locker rooms, hold their hands when a mother or father died, applaud them when they came up with questions that stumped me, kneel beside them in prayer, tell them all my corny jokes, rejoice with them over the girls who loved them.

Those thoughts ran through my mind, becoming more and more vivid as the time drew close. They became expectations. Those same beautiful dreams that made my kids come alive for me before I even met them became restrictions after school started, and made my kids less real.

My expectations for my kids all too often tempted me to mold them into the way I wanted them to be. The dreams, hopes and wishes that I had for them before we met frequently became demands after school started. This was not malicious. I didn't do it consciously, deliberately. I had no intention of hurting them. Instead I had convinced myself that what I ambitioned for them was in their own best interests. It was because I cared so much for them! Yet, when I cared in that way, I didn't face and enjoy each boy as he really was.

Our expectations for our children may be good ones. The point is not whether they are good or misguided or evil. That's not it at all. The point is that our expectations mold our present decisions. They affect our reactions and strongly influence our present relationship with our children.

No one's asking anyone to give up his expectations. What has to go is our commitment to the expectations. We can become so absorbed in our expectations that we lose sight of the child. A ballplayer who's obsessed with major league baseball may want to train his boy—no matter what—to be a major leaguer. The expectation of the major leagues is not wrong; it's letting it become so important that the boy is missed.

We may not see ourselves as unduly determined in our expectations. We see ourselves as reasonable and prudent. After all, our expectations are similar to those of the other parents we know. Of course we feel education is important. But we can be obsessed with education just as much as a father can be obsessed with baseball.

What is the effect of expectations on your relationship with your children?

Your answer:

We might have great expectations for all of our children. They might be next to impossible to fulfill, demanding each child's total involvement of time or energy or talent. With such high demands we probably have an interior radar that keeps us fixed on the ultimate goal, correcting our course any time there's a sign of veering off. It makes us crystal ball gazers, because we're constantly peering into the future.

There's also the possibility that we have great expectations for one or two of our children and little or no expectations for the others. That means some get too much attention and some get too little.

A lot of factors go into the disparity in our expectations. One is age. The most is usually expected of the eldest child. Another factor is intelligence. We might agree that one of our children is the one for whom we have the highest hopes. We think that he is the brightest or the most talented or has had the best exposure to education.

At the opposite end of the scale is the child from whom we don't expect much. We estimate that he's not blessed with brains.

Another factor is sex. Today we are especially aware of how the potential of women had been reduced by limiting their opportunities to develop their capabilities. We haven't yet come to grips with how sharply we've limited men! We don't expect very much from them in terms of personal relationships.

Other factors which cause our expectations to vary from child to child are the order of appearance in the family and physical or personal attractiveness.

Our expectations are also conditioned by what we're told to expect from boys, from girls, from two-year olds, from teenagers. We become prejudiced. Told about the terrible twos, we expect our child of two to be a lot of trouble. On the other hand, five is supposed to be a nice age, so we look for our five-year-old to be placid. It would be better to ask ourselves how much the child's activities are conditioned by our expectations! Do we create an atmosphere of expecting too much? If so, pleasing us is not a joy but a burden. Demands that are too high put the child in a prison and restrict his freedom. The children then exist for our sake, for the gratification of our expectations.

Cathy is a gorgeous girl with long black hair, dimples, and she's sixteen. I've known her since she was six. I used to bounce her on my knee, read her stories when I tucked her in at night, take her to the circus, swim in the surf—oh, we were great friends. We had long talks about anything and everything and I just enjoyed whatever it pleased her to talk about. Then she became a teen-ager!

Gradually walls started to come up between us. I wondered what had happened to that little girl who would wait at the door for me when I visited the family and throw herself into my arms. I understood, you just don't act the same way when you get to be a big girl, but she didn't seem to care whether I came over or not. (I got in some good digs about that, but it didn't help). I really missed her warmth. I didn't tell her that. Instead, I told her she should greet me because I thought it was only right that she should.

When we did talk, she seemed to be like any other teenager. Her ideas were so mixed up! I tried to straighten her out, but everything I said just seemed to start an argument. I felt she had to change. She couldn't get her way every time she pleased. She had to know she was wrong. Frequently I thought she was very disrespectful.

One day she yelled at me, "I hate you." After all I had done for her! It wasn't so bad when she was a little girl. I could laugh it off knowing we'd be friends again in no time. But now it really hurt. I couldn't forget it. When I visited, we either seemed to ignore each other, were very polite or I got into an argument with her. She had always listened to me. Now when it was so much more important, she just seemed to do as she pleased.

One day I was trying to get her to see that she had to do better. She burst into tears and said, "Father Chuck, I wish you'd re- member a little more of when you were growing up and demand a little less." Suddenly it hit me. Cathy had changed, yes, but I had

There's a drum major to be proud of.
He leads the family fun.

changed even more! Before, I had enjoyed her. Now, I was expecting all sorts of things from her. I was seeing her as a typical teen instead of Cathy. The enormity of what I had done belted me between the eyes. I felt so small, so cruel. I had been holding her for damns instead of holding *her*, appreciating *her*.

Now I'm learning. I'm looking at her enthusiasm and goodness. I'm clamping down on my mouth and doing a lot more listening and discovering that she's a very remarkable young lady!

To see where we are, let's write out what our expectations are for each child. That will tell us about our relationships. It might be painful to look into this honestly and sincerely, but we need to recognize what we are doing to our children.

What do your expectations for your children reveal about you?

Your answer:

Our expectations reveal what our values and goals are. After all, we want for our children what is worthwhile to us. We may not have achieved it. We may have settled for something less because of circumstances beyond our control. Or, maybe we were attracted to something more meaningful to us at the time, such as an early marriage.

When we concentrate on our expectations we don't really enjoy our children. We are only concerned with their performance and behavior. We get into a teacher-pupil relationship, always pointing the way and helping the children do the correct thing. We miss the special joy we can have as parents. As parents, we have the opportunity to help them to experience us in the closest relationship on earth.

How many of our expectations are only concerned with what our children will do in later life? What success they're going to achieve? What their relationships are going to be with other people? How much happiness they will achieve because of those successes, those activities, or those other relationships. All of this is good, but it indicates a guardian or custodial role. Someone other than a parent could have those expectations.

What we expect of our children could also indicate what we once expected of each other, but now know we won't receive—at least in the fullest measure. Just as we might try to make our son or daughter into the person we didn't become, so too we might try to make our children into the person that our spouse didn't become!

Or have we seen the flaws and failures in our marriage and now expect our children to give us the satisfactions we haven't achieved?

Our harmony as a couple can be seen by how similar our expectations are for our children. If our expectations differ very much we have disharmony in our husband-wife relationship. We may have learned to be fairly subtle on this unfortunate battleground and not openly engage in a tug-of-war. But in our minds and hearts we're going in conflicting directions. It can be different, for one of the beautiful things about marriage is that the man and woman can gradually assume common goals which override any individual goal they may have.

Also, by looking at what we expect of our children, we can measure how realistic we are as parents. We may over- or underestimate our child's potential because of the way we see ourselves. If we see ourselves as untalented or not having used our talents, then we tend to exaggerate our children's capabilities or incapabilities.

A father's failure in not having lettered in high school may drive him to push his son into spending his whole childhood on sports. He may relive through that child what he missed in his childhood. Furthermore, he may see his own life as dull and doesn't want that for his boy.

We may do the same thing regarding popularity, education, money, religion, discipline, etc. Or we may go in the opposite direction. We may be very strict or very lenient. The point is that we're responding to what *we* resented when *we* were growing up, what *we* dreamed of, what *we* thought we were deprived of. If we see this we can do something about the expectations we have for our children.

We need to ask ourselves what our capabilities were, what talents we had. We often look back on the days of our youth with rose-colored glasses and say, "Well, if I had studied harder I'd have done better." We should begin realizing that we probably did as well as we could considering our talents. Our dream or ideal is unrealistic because we never honestly assessed our capabilities.

The next step is to assess the child's capabilities. They may be less or greater than our own. Either is difficult to accept. It's hard to admit that our child is not bright. It's harder to admit he is more talented than we are. A superior child threatens us. We tend to act defensively. We may make more and more demands of the child in the same area of his interest or in other areas in order for us to evade the child's superiority.

How do your expectations affect your child's self-image?

Your answer:

We often ask our children to live up to an ideal that comes from within us rather than from within them. Our ideal was likely formed before they were born. Subtly and implicitly we tell them that their worth and goodness is dependent upon how closely they approximate our dream child. No matter how hard he tries or how sincerely he works, it's impossible for him to live up to that dream, so our son or daughter develops a strong sense of failure. He sees himself as definitely not the person he ought to be.

Every child, for a period of time, attempts to respond to what his parents want. If he constantly fails to live up to that standard, the child gives up. This leads to friction between the child and his parents and, consequently, to the child's feeling guilty from a sense of having let his parents down.

Our expectations become imbued in our children whether or not they live up to them. The child compares himself with our expectations and always comes up short. This problem is a double one. Although our ideal is good in itself, the child sees himself as bad because he's not accomplishing it. Too, a boy or girl recognizes that this is what his mother and father want for him. He loves his mother and father dearly and knows they are good people. He wants to please them, and when he fails it isn't just failing to live up to an ideal; it's failing to live up to his *parents'* ideal.

This whole thing focused for me when my expectations ran over Ronnie. He was a boy in one of my classes—a great kid—bright, an honorable-mention student and one of those boys that's good, full of integrity, willing and eager to please. He was a little quiet, though, and I thought if I got him into some school activity, it would do him good. I talked him into being in a play. I was quite pleased with myself. This was just what he needed. It would force him to come out of himself.

I almost destroyed that beautiful boy. After 3 weeks he was a nervous wreck; his marks plummeted; the strain showed on his face. He was trying so hard to live up to what I expected of him that it was too much for him. His mom and dad tried to get him out of dramatics, but he didn't want to let me down. When he finally did leave, he looked on himself as a failure and he was sure I did too! He had to transfer to another class. . . . I had lost a friend.

How do your expectations affect your self-image as parents?

As good parents we want to be happy, but when our children can't live up to our expectations, their sense of failure communicates itself to us. We can do one of two things: communicate the ideal more clearly or re-examine the ideal. We'll make more progress by doing the latter. We might see the ideal isn't custom-made for each child, that it's centered in our own head and heart. The ideal is not bad in itself, it's bad when it's forced on any of our children. We need to face that reality. If we don't the unhappiness of each child grows and so does our own.

Good parents want what is best for their children, but parents don't know ahead of time what that is. Yet when our expectations don't work out, our self-image suffers. We see ourselves as having let our children down, as having failed.

Jim was a big lanky kid who loved basketball. The only reason he liked school at all was because he was on the team. Every six weeks when the report card came home it was a big hassle because Jim did far better on the court than he did in the classroom. It upset his parents because they worried about what he was going to do with his life if he didn't get good marks. But it was like walking in a field of melted marshmallows trying to get Jim to study. He made all sorts of promises, but nothing ever changed. He was All-City in basketball and at the bottom of his class in school. This continued through college. He was a good boy and his parents loved him dearly, but what was he going to do? He couldn't play basketball all his life. They felt they had failed.

Jim really surprised them. After college he settled down, got a job, went to night school for his master's degree and got B+'s. They couldn't believe it. This couldn't be their Jim! But it was! He found a good job, married and had a great family—with a kid who drives him up the wall because he loves basketball so much.

One of the problems is that we equate our expectations with

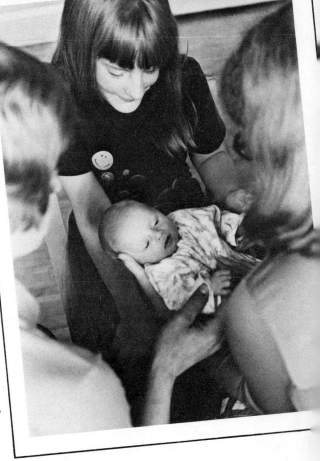

Will he be like Mom? Like Dad? Whatever the future holds he'll be an expression of their love — like me.

our values. Thinking of them as the same thing, we believe that each time our children don't live up to our expectations they are rejecting our values. And because our values are a part of us it's as though our children are rejecting us.

We may give up trying to communicate with our children or become so insistent upon the living out of the expectations as our values that we cause a breach between us. Or we can create a situation of détente. They have their values and we have ours. In any case, the way we see ourselves is negative.

The call for parents is to discover the goodness in their children, to draw it out and amplify it, rather than to impose it on them. If we make our children's goodness something they have to become rather than who they are, or if we make their activities the source of their goodness rather than an expression of it, we make them into whom we want them to be, rather than in rejoicing in who they are. They will experience a great deal of unhappiness and we'll look on ourselves as poor parents. Actually, the problem is not the children, it's not us, it's our expectations.

A coach matches the system to his team, not the other way around. He may prefer a team that fastbreaks, but if he doesn't have the players who can do it, he has to work out a more set offensive for them. If he keeps expecting the team to fastbreak he will lose a lot of games and alienate his players from him. They and he will be unhappy.

What is being a parent all about?

Your answer:

Basically a child is a specific precious expression of a husband and wife's love for each other. The child is unique and irreplaceable. In a special way he speaks the love his parents have for each other.

The main job of parents is to speak to and listen, not so much to what the child says, as to who the child is. In that way they discover more about their love for each other.

Too often we treat the child as separate and distinct from the husband-and-wife relationship. Actually the greatest glory of the child is that he is a fulfillment of his parents' relationship. By his very existence he speaks the meaning and glory of that relationship. Therefore parents ought to discover the child's specific capabilities, talents and goodnesses, not only for the sake of the child, but also for the sake of their relationship. By who he is, the child will reveal dimensions of the husband and wife's relationship his parents could never discover by themselves. If we don't let our child be himself and if we keep telling him who he has to become, then we miss discovering our full selves and our love.

Jerry looked on himself as a sharp business man. He had built a big company because he was a hard driver who pushed a tough bargain. Marcia saw herself as a liberated woman, sophisticated and independent. She took the lead in every group she joined. They couldn't figure out their children. They were so opposite. Every one of them was softspoken, gentle and kind. Jerry and Marcia wondered if somebody had made a mistake in the hospital and switched the babies around! The truth of the matter was that their children were a reflection of the way Jerry and Marcia were with each other. They were different people in the home and the children had breathed in that atmosphere. They didn't see themselves as having the qualities of softness and tenderness until they saw it in their children.

For some reason we often look on parenthood as distinct from marriage. Of course we know marriage is a necessary precondition for parenthood, but do we consider it so for social acceptability or because we believe that marriage is necessary to properly support and raise a child? Either reason undersells the depth, intimacy and importance of the child to the husband-and-wife relationship.

A child is created because of what a man and woman think of each other, what they are determined to be to each other, and because of the commitment of their relationship for the years to come. A child is more than a commitment to take care of. He is a gift that I give to and receive from my beloved. Not only in the moment of conception, but in his continuing life.

The real meaning of parenthood, then, is for a husband and wife to discover themselves in their child. The child makes them more aware of each other and their love and speaks to them in his existence.

When we make our parenthood a separate relationship from our marriage, we focus in on expectations for the child, especially future expectations. Oh yes, we recognize that the child comes about as a result of our marriage and that we have a mutual responsibility. It's our responsibility toward each other, not toward the child, that is what parenthood is all about.

We'll live in the present with our children and be less burdened by the future if, in husband-and-wife relationship, we see our children as an expression of our love for each other. If our love is consciously and deliberately expressed in the home now, then our children will have a successful life because they have experienced being loved along with being provided for.

There are three basic motivations for loving a child. The child can be loved in himself. The child can be loved as "mine." The child can be loved as my beloved's and mine—"ours." If the child is loved directly in himself, then the love is conditioned in terms of how much that child pleases me. If the child is loved as "my" child, then the love is centered in me. In both cases, the roots, the source of the child, namely our love for each other, is absent. On the other hand when the child is loved as a direct expression of the husband's and wife's love for each other, the child is irreplaceable and invaluable.

So, to be parents, is to love the child not only by making sure he's properly equipped and prepared to live life, but to let the child know that he is essential to the couple relationship. Then the child has a full meaning and identity from the first moment of his existence. The child's identity and meaning is not dependent on his reaching maturity. He always has a total value because his existence speaks of the relationship as husband and wife. As he grows and his capabilities develop, then he's more able to express his value.

In folklore there's always been a specialness ascribed to the loved child. Whenever a man and woman were overwhelmingly in love at the time the child was conceived, he had such a magnificent start he had to be unique. It is not only the beginning that makes the difference, it's the continuing relationship between that man and woman that the child infuses. The best parent is overwhelmingly in love with his husband or wife.

Yes, every child should be conceived and born of a tremendous love affair but, more importantly, he should be raised in one.

The more we treat the child as an isolated, separate individual, the more we fail as parents. We distort the reality of who that child is. He should not be alone "out there." He is "us." He is our love, living and breathing, with a name. It is not only our past love but our present love that the child is expressing as he grows and achieves a greater consciousness and awareness. Therefore, it is important for a husband and wife to see each other and their relationship as it is inherent in all the interaction they have with their child.

What are your children saying of your relationship? Not in the words he is using but in his experience of his personhood. The ability of children to relate to themselves is greatly determined by how a husband and wife are relating. A child's self-acceptance is strongly conditioned by his parents' acceptance of each other. His joy in life is sharply affected by how much joy his mother and father find in each other.

We recognize that an orphan has a difficult time. But we often treat our children as orphans. Being without a father and mother is difficult, not just because the child needs a masculine and feminine influence, but because the child's identity is in question. The child can't see the fullness of who he is when his parents are missing. However, this can also be true when both parents are in the home but are dealing with the child outside of their couple-

Mom and Dad were great in high school — dramatics and sports. But we can beat them at chess!

ness. They can be seeming to do all the right things and even pride themselves on letting their child be his own self, but they are depriving him if they're treating the child as someone apart. The basic roots for any of us is our parents' love for each other. Showing forth our love for each other is one of the most important ways to get across to our child that we love him.

And the most valuable thing we can teach our children is *how to love*. Being able to relate positively to other human beings is an essential dimension of any person's fullness in life. We want a full life for our children. Our children will be able to relate more meaningfully to others if they recognize that they are a living, breathing expression of our relationship with each other. The child is our love incarnate. They are a continuing memorial of our love. Our child's whole being expresses now and forevermore, "us." Consequently, we have to make "us" present to them even when we deal individually with them.

**Is a relationship
taught or experienced?**

Your answer:

We can talk about our relationship to the children, but that isn't enough. They have to experience it. They can experience it when we're together and also when only one of us is with them. Our husband-and-wife relationship can be just as present when only one of us is with the children as when we are both with them.

A father can deal with a son or daughter not only as "his" but as "hers" and "theirs." A mother can't be just taking care of "her" children. She needs to be responding to their needs because of her love for her husband, their father. Our love for each other can be so real and vibrant that the children breathe it in the air of our home.

This is a wonderful thing for children. They don't have to

perform, they don't have to live up to a lot of expectations, they don't have to possess impressive talents and abilities. Their reason for existence is because of our great love. Then there is no pressure on the children—they don't have to earn our respect or our love. They are loved in a love that existed before they were born and continues to exist—our marital love. In no greater measure can a child experience being valued, appreciated, reverenced or cared for.

We can explain to our children the intellectual concepts of how to get along with others, be prepared for marriage, have deep friendships, but unless they experience our husband-and-wife relationship in the fullest measure now, their own relationships in years to come will be crippled. They'll be looking for a mother or a father to take care of them rather than wanting to participate in a couple relationship.

On the other hand, if they have a meaning from the first moment of their existence, they will be able to engage in a deep, meaningful interpersonal relationship. And they will always be a celebration of us and our love for each other. There's no living in the future in this type of relationship. There's no waiting for the child to grow up to be somebody. He is already somebody! This avoids the separation that frequently occurs after the child attains maturity. He has had identity from the first moment of his existence. He hasn't had to find an identity in the things he does to live up to our expectations. When a child has to continually try to meet our expectations in order to "belong," in later years he will take his own expectations, split off from us and do the things that please him.

All through life our child should remind us of each other. Not only in the external sense that he walks the way his father does, or she has the same pattern of speech as her mother. But whenever we see our children, we should be reminded of our love. The similarities of face, figure and characteristics make each other present and remind us of how much we love and are loved.

A child who grows up in this kind of atmosphere is a lucky child. There is no responsibility on him to earn love. A child instinctively asks, "Why do my mother and father make all these sacrifices for me, take on the burden of raising me, spend their whole life centered around me?" There is no adequate answer. The only satisfying kind of answer is, "We do this because of our love for each other," "Your father is my whole life!" "You are my beloved's gift to me."

Something wonderful happens when a family enjoys this atmosphere. They don't concentrate on children, preparing them for the future, expecting great things of them in the years to come. The mother and father don't look to them for their satisfaction or fullness in life. The couple lives in the present with their children.

A couple doesn't have to worry about their children making it in this world or whether or not they are properly equipped to make a living or be a success. If sons and daughters are presently expressing who we are to each other accurately, meaningfully and fully, we will be content.

What are our children expressing now? It is whatever our relationship is with each other. If they or we are not happy, we may have to change, not them. Often when we're dissatisfied with the children, we want them to change. Other times, we may see that as parents we need to change. But there's an even more important relationship to check out. How is our husband-and-wife relationship? Is there a deficiency there? We may need to improve the atmosphere of love we're generating with each other.

Whenever our children begin to upset us in one way or another, then we ought to look at how we're relating to our spouse. We can be confident that if the husband-and-wife relationship is open, communicative, responsive, tender and thoughtful, the children will reflect that. If the husband-and-wife relationship is closed, cold, hard and unkind, the children will reflect that in selfishness, hostility, withdrawal, or in not exercising their talents.

It's hard to face the reality of our being on the wrong track. It's easier to put the responsibility on the children to shape up, or even to acknowledge our involvement by wondering how we can get across to them or how we can relate better to them. What we need to see is how we can be relating better to our husband or wife! That's where the answer lies. All the beautiful things we do for our children are going to be undercut unless our prime relationship is strong, sturdy, faithful and loving.

It's not simply that we should improve our marital relationship because it improves our parental role. No, but if we lose sight of our relationship as married people, we lose sight of the children as *our* children. They become little people to take care of and provide for. Maybe we love that burden and are satisfied to live with it, but nonetheless it is a burden. If we get our focus corrected, we'll discover fantastic new joys in parenting.

How do your spouse's expectations compare with yours?

Your answer:

If we have talked in depth about how we see our children, what we expect from them, the dreams and nightmares we have concerning them, we'll know each other's feelings.

However, one's convictions and desires may be so intense that he doesn't stop to find out whether or not his dream might be the other's nightmare. He doesn't imagine his spouse wanting anything different. Differences in expectations lead to misunderstanding and friction between a husband and wife—and between them and the children. If I have specific ambitions for the children, and those of my spouse are not the same, I'll be disturbed. I'll think he is not supporting me, that he is lessening the chance of the children's future happiness, that there's a danger the children won't work toward my goals—or will try to attain his rather than mine.

As a consequence, coolness or distrust can grow in our relationship. The children become a battlefield where we struggle to get our own ways. In such circumstances, I judge the goodness, worth and effectiveness of my spouse in terms of whether or not he has the same expectations I have, and whether or not he is getting them across as I want or don't want him to.

When I do this, I'm perceiving the children in a way far less than what it can or should be. I'm seeing the children as for my sake, rather than as an expression of our husband-and-wife relationship. I cut them off from the richness of "us."

Sometimes we might want the same thing, but for entirely

different reasons. To one a college education might be a symbol of success. For the other, it might be a sign of social status. We assume we have good reasons and that they are valid ones. On closer examination one's motive may be the prestige it gives, the others, the money it may bring the children. So the first thing we have to do is discover the differences in our expectations for our children. After all, during the years before we met, many ideals, hopes and dreams as well as fears became ingrained in each of us. They don't automatically become our joint feelings.

We have to ask some questions. What does "happy" mean to each of us? How would you ensure that the children are happy? How would I? What would indicate their happiness to you—to me—now and in later life? What is a good family life? What would you like to see in our children's marital relationships and their relationships with their children? What does getting ahead mean? A lot of money? A profession? What profession? What are the differences in either of our minds between a teacher and a doctor, a musician and a ball player?

It's vital to spell out the details in order to discover where we differ in our expectations. The next step is to start talking about the values these expectations represent. Our expectations are based on the values we hold dear. Perhaps we've not verbalized them before. When we begin to put them into words and come to grips with what values we're protecting and trying to inculcate in our children, then we have a chance to be one in mind and heart in transmitting them.

Our expectations reveal the values we really have. We may believe we have humanistic values that we want to transmit to our children, when actually the expectations are materialistic. For instance, we may say we are concerned for our fellowman and believe in helping people so it is our ambition that our child become a doctor. It's a people-helping profession. But deep in our hearts we like the idea that he'll make a great deal of money. If we don't want that same child to be a nurse or a para-medic (because he won't make that much money), our true value is showing.

The opposite may sometimes occur, because we're trained in our society to be practical. Our spiritual and humanistic values may be expressed in pragmatic terms in order that our husband or wife will not think of us as dreamers. For example, I may say our son should be a doctor—because he'll make plenty of money and be secure—when I'm really caring more about his serving mankind.

It's a good idea for husband and wife to take the time to sit down and dig deep within each other to discover the motivation behind their expectations for their children. They also have to discover what effect those different expectations have on their relationship. It may be that one is practical and so are his values. The other partner—and his values—may be more idealistic. In all probability, in their relationship with their children they have been correcting each other. The practical one doesn't want the children carried away by the dream world of the husband or wife. The idealistic one is fearful that the children will be too pragmatic. This is not a parental problem; it is a marital one. The husband and wife need to integrate each other's values into their "couple" life. They need a unit—a common set of values to share with their children.

Jackie and Fred had a heated argument one night over whether or not to send their young son Jimmy to camp. Jackie thought Fred was being very selfish, that he just wanted to get rid of the boy so that he could have a free summer. Fred was equally upset at Jackie. He thought that she was being a smothering mother. They went back and forth, putting words into each other's mouth and assuming that they knew the motivation behind the other person's position.

Finally, Jackie said "Look, let's stop hurling accusations and forget camp for a minute. Let's just the two of us talk about what we want for our son," Fred explained to her how important it was for him to give the boy freedom, an opportunity to make his own decisions and to have friends of his own. He wanted Jim to have some breathing room, an opportunity to make mistakes without having them corrected right away.

Jackie wanted to make sure that Jimmy knew how much he was loved and wanted by them. She wanted him to go into adult life with a lot of fond memories of being with the family. It was very important to her that Jimmy have time with his father during the summertime when his father had a little more time to spend with him.

When they had finished explaining their values to each other, both were surprised to recognize that there wasn't a single thing that either one objected to. It wasn't a matter of having different values. They just had a different priority on those values. The next thing was to develop couple values. It meant asking, "Which one of the two of us at this moment is most capable of taking on the other person's values?" It meant reaching out and adopting as one's own, the value of the other person. It wasn't easy, but it took a lot of friction out of their lives and they're much more united as a couple in their relationship with Jimmy.

We may kid ourselves and say, "If the children get both sets of values they can choose and get a good mix." No, they get confused. The two people they love most dearly present two different plans of life. The child is torn. He wants to please both parents, but can't because there are two conflicting ambitions. If he chooses one, he's on one parent's side. If he chooses the other, he's on the other's side. What the child tends to do is choose neither.

Better than spelling out the ambitions we have for our children, we should have them experience our values. Then they should be allowed to choose the way to express those values themselves. They will be a unique expression of our love.

Values are precious things a husband and wife give to each other. They are what makes life worthwhile. We may believe material and social values deserve less emphasis than spiritual, psychologial or personal values, but each has meaning. We need to find the goodness of each other's values and take those values on in addition to our own. We enrich each other. Our common values become a dowry.

In the husband-and-wife relationship, we strive for what's meaningful to the other person. This is true with values. What is "valuable" to you means something to me. I give my values to my beloved, not because mine are right and yours are wrong, but because I want to share this richness with the one I love. My money, my education, my social position, my friends, or whatever, can't be kept to myself if I'm a married person. And it's selfish to give them with the attitude that they are mine, but I'll let you use them. The fullness of a couple's giving is for each to take on the other's values as his own. Your likes, my likes, become *our* likes. Your friends, my friends, become *our* friends.

Do you realize the extent of your expectations?   *Your answer:*

When we impose our expectations on our children, they grow up trying to live them out. We get the worst of both worlds. As they grow, we're living 20 years in the future. When they are grown, they live 20 years in the past. We all miss the present. That is a horror, isn't it?

This is not an exaggeration. After 21 years of living in an atmosphere in which a certain set of goals is held out to them, it's going to be very difficult for them to act on them. Either positively—they'll keep working toward them; or negatively—they'll reject the goal and make most of their decisions in life going against it. The way the child lives is determined by our goals even though it appears he is making his own decisions.

It is better that we give our child values! Then he can make his own decisions as to the best way to express them. If we give him specific goals, we take away his freedom and deprive him of a beautiful part of us.

What is it we want for our children? What is it that is the best thing for them? Not to be just like one of us—or even like the best in each of us! No, the most important thing is that they express fully and meaningfully who *we* are and continue to be to each other.

The happiness, the fullness, the success of our parent-child relationship is based on the degree to which we're experiencing our precious gift of each other—and passing it on to them!

We love each other — and the outdoors. May she know both.

Do your children a favor.
Begin to see what really
good parents you are!

2

PARENT-IMAGE

Do you often evaluate yourself as a parent?

Your answer:

We all hope that we're good parents. But to keep on being good parents, it is important that we stop every once in a while and look at ourselves. How are we doing? How effective are we with our children? If we never or seldom evaluate ourselves, we're like a doctor who always thinks of himself in terms of how well he did in medical school. (He may not keep up with the developments in the medical professions—and not be as good a doctor as he thinks he is!)

At first we felt good about our parenting when we kept our

baby well fed, dry and smiling. As the years go by and the family increases, we gain new insights on parenthood. We have new norms by which to evaluate ourselves. There are many changes, and our children have different personalities. We can ask, "Is my parental rating the same with all the children or different with each one? At this moment, maybe we would rate ourselves as good parents with our oldest and average or poor parents with the others—or vice versa. How do we arrive at our conclusions?

On what do you base your evaluation?   *Your answer:*

Often we use other people's norms to measure our effectiveness with our children. For instance we may follow some book or newspaper or magazine columns on raising children and use that as our measuring stick.

Or we compare our children with other children. We get it into our heads that at a certain age a child should begin to walk or talk or eat with a spoon or ride a bicycle.

We may predecide what school marks our children ought to get, or how many friends they should have. So, if our children fit the concept we have, we rate ourselves as good parents.

Maybe we judge our parenthood in terms of the affection our children show us. If our children are responding to us with warmth, then we approve of ourselves as parents. Or our judgment may be based on obedience. If we're having difficulties with getting our children to bed, to do their homework or to take care of their rooms, we grade ourselves as poor parents.

Discipline is another area by which we judge ourselves as parents. We may think we are being "too strict" or "too lenient"—or "just right."

Young parents tend to look for immediate results rather than seeing their parenthood as a long-term thing. They expect to be effective immediately. If they aren't, they feel inadequate.

Some parents rank themselves in terms of the skills—mechanical, educational or social—their children develop. If they see that the children are progressing well for their ages, then they rate themselves as satisfactory parents. (That raises an interesting question. Is parenthood a job?)

Another basis for judging ourselves as parents can be on skills that we think good parents should have. We might be able to plan nutritious meals, help with schoolwork, play ball, be patient, help them with practicing their music and so on. Each skill has little to do with the relationship we have with our children. Parents who have none of those skills could be excellent because of how real they are to their children. And the parents who have all those skills could be poor parents because they are strangers to their children. We know that everybody has different talents, so not every parent can perform the same services for his children.

Rather than evaluating our parenthood by how our children act, how much they accomplish or achieve, or what skills we have, it is better to evaluate our parenting by what our relationship with them is.

Are we aware of them as persons? Are they aware of us as persons? Are we "close" to them? Do we know each one in terms of what he is feeling and what is important to him? Are they experiencing us on a deep level? Are they able to communicate with us meaningfully and openly? Are they able to really listen to us—not only in terms of obedience but in terms of touching our personhood and experiencing who we are?

Most of us recognize the importance of human beings being able to relate well to each other, but we are apt to believe other things are more important. We care deeply about our children's education, their health care and the development of their talents. And we often overlook our relationship with them. We think it will grow apace as we take care of the other areas. Actually the reverse is true. If we develop a deep personal relationship with our children, the other things will take care of themselves or be taken care of far more easily than if we don't. A child can learn to walk, talk, develop motor skills, go to school, get good marks and have an adequate number of playmates, but if he doesn't develop a close relationship with his parents, all the other is not enough.

So we need to ask ourselves, "How much do our children know about us? How much do they empathize with what's important to us?" Of course, we should take into account each child's age and maturity, but these capabilities are probably more developed than we imagine. Let's ask, too, "How much do we allow the children to respond to us and make a contribution to our lives?" In terms of understanding and heart-to-heart communication, maybe we've not let each child speak out freely on what is going on inside him. We always are correcting, instructing, counselling or advising him! How free are the children to be themselves? Do they always have to perform correctly or live up to certain expectations that we have?

We're going to be parents to our children all their lives long, and obedience and authority will be a small part of our parent-child relationship, especially when they are adults. They should not be insisted upon at the expense of our relationship with one another.

The real test of our rating as parents might be summed up in one question. Do they love us and do we love them? Love isn't a one-way street. Love isn't a relationship in which one party, the parent, does everything for the other, the child. It is one in which both parties are mutually responsive. Naturally children are dependent for a while, but as the child grows up he should be encouraged to become increasingly equal to the parent in terms of the relationship.

We like to give our children pleasant memories. Our method is often to allow privileges and give good times. We also want to prepare them to get more education and a job, so we discipline them. These are aspects of raising a child. But these wonderful and important things—don't necessarily have to be done by a parent.

What's the difference between being a parent and being a person who is raising children? Raising children stops when the children reach a certain age or achieve a necessary level of competence. Raising children is a limited and temporary job. *Parenthood is forever.* The raising of the child is not the focus of parenthood. It's a result, but what is most valuable is the extent of the parent-child interaction. To evaluate what that is, we need to look at the love between us. Not how much have I done for my children, but what kind of love do we have for one another? In order to love, we have to know. So the level of our knowing one another is the measure of our love. That is the measuring stick to use as we evaluate ourselves as parents.

Our children have difficulty knowing us if we hold back from them. We hold back in many ways. We don't want them to know we have doubts about anything for fear it will interfere with our authority. We don't want to say, "I'm sorry," to the children, because we think it's going to undercut their being obedient to us. However, if we want our children to love us, they need to know the reality of us. If we let them know our real selves, then their love can be real. If we live out the role of "parent" rather than just being the person we are, we can expect a certain amount of appreciation and respect for our dutifulness and self-sacrifice, but the area of a true-love relationship is missing.

Jean felt she wasn't a good mother until recently. She told me how frustrated she used to get. "When the kids had been fighting, or one of them had been stealing from the corner grocery store, or supper wasn't ready, or all three happened at once, I complained, sometimes I griped, sometimes I gave orders, sometimes I cried, but mostly I hurt—and it was all done in the name of Motherhood. Surely if I were a good mother, they wouldn't fight or steal and I'd have the meal on time!

The children are married— but never gone to us— and now we can look forward to grand- children!

51

"Now I'm learning to drop my mask of Mother. I'm daring to explain my real feelings. When I actually reveal my true self and trust that the family will love me anyway, everything is better. Each time I tell the kids of bad things I've done and the rotten feelings I have, I feel I'm taking a risk. It's like putting my head on the guillotine block and trusting that the masked man will not chop. But I'm doing it and learning that the children recognize me more and more as a person and accept me and forgive me and love me. It's pure joy."

How big a part does taking care of our children play in our lives? How big a part do our children, themselves, play in our lives? There's a big difference. Our whole life can center around doing things for our children and yet we can miss knowing them. We may be busy with them and yet not be in their lives or they in ours. The important thing is to give of ourselves to the fullest of our ability so that our relationship is rich. Our relationship is going to exist all our life long. We will always be parents to our children—as we are always children to our parents. And our children will always be our children even when they are parents to their children. What will vary according to age and circumstance is how our relationships are expressed. In later life our children may have to take care of us. If that caring is the fulfilling of a duty, then it's going to be degrading. If it's an expression of our love for one another, we can accept that service as an expression of love.

How do you evaluate your spouse as a parent?

Your answer:

We have probably formed some sort of judgment as to what kind of parent our spouse is. And that judgment is likely colored by how we judge ourselves. If we have a high opinion of our spouse, it may make us look bad, and if we have a low opinion, it may make us look good as a parent but bad as a marriage partner. Just as we need to evaluate our effectiveness as parents at various times, so we need to reevaluate our spouse as a parent. Maybe we presume that because a man disliked changing diapers, he can't be a good father of teenagers. Or, because a woman lost her temper with pre-schoolers she must, therefore, be an unsatisfactory mother of school-age children. Let's forget the past and evaluate our spouse in terms of the present. Who is our spouse to the children at this particular time?

How I evaluate my spouse as a parent affects the way I act. If I think that he is unusually good, I may put myself down or try to become like him. I may even give up in those areas of our relationship with our children where I think he is better. I may think he is more consistent, more gentle and more understanding than I am, so I back off.

On the other hand, if I think my husband or wife is a rather poor parent, I may try to compensate for it. I may become very strict to make up for the other's leniency. Or, the opposite, I may let the children's little peccadillos slide by so the other's stern discipline won't be aroused.

We should also consider what part we played in making our spouse the way he is. Maybe we took over the interaction with the children and he was pushed out.

The purpose of parents evaluating each other is not to change either one. The purpose is to find unity. It's vitally important to our children and ourselves that we be consistent, not only in terms of supporting each other, but by being of one mind and heart.

It's of vital importance that our children respond to us as a couple. They can only do that if we are "one." We need to be aware of what our values are, and what is dear to each of our hearts about our children. Then the children will not face us as two separate individuals but as a couple.

I may think my beloved is an exceptional parent and lead him to believe he can never fail. I'm putting him in the position of always having to live up to that role. I make it hard for him to have any doubts or difficulties and to discuss them. I've made him perfect. The reason behind that could be to take the burden off myself. One perfect person in the home is enough!

On the other hand, I may be so negative about my spouse's dealings with the children that he loses all self-confidence and doesn't want to do anything with them for fear of being criticized.

There is also a middle-of-the-road position. I may not voice any opinions about my husband's or wife's capability as a parent. It is a protective device in that if I don't criticize him, he can't criticize me. It results in our having no rapport with each other over the children. We're not letting them be *our* children. They're yours, when you're dealing with them; they're mine, when I'm dealing with them. No one really wants that, but if a husband or a wife tries to make the other person more like himself, parenthood becomes more of a source of dissension. Forcing a change doesn't work. It leads to confrontation or to withdrawal, with the statement, "Take care of it yourself!" It may lead to a division of responsibilities in which each of us has his own sphere of influence.

If either of us evaluates the other negatively as a parent, then this has to be talked about. The best way is to find out what our values are in regard to our children. Once we've seen what is in each other's heart and mind and accepted each other's values, we can relate to the children not as two singles with a mutual interest, but as a couple!

On what do you base your evaluation?

Your answer:

I usually evaluate my spouse as I do myself—on the basis of books I have read, the expectations I have for our children or what I have decided is the proper role of a father or mother. As a result, I'm measuring my spouse by my measuring stick. I box him in the same way I've boxed in myself.

The basis of judgment should be on how much of a personal relationship does my beloved and our children have with one another—how well they know each other. I may be jealous of that relationship. I may see it as taking away from me. I may see the burden of raising children all on me, whereas he has it the easy way. The truth is that *raising children is the easy way*. The difficult way, but the best and most rewarding way for everyone, is for each parent to be a person, not somebody playing a role, and for them to allow their children to be persons to them.

In your evaluation do you make comparisons?

Your answer:

Comparisons are odious and yet we make them all the time. It's an easy thing to make comparisons when we evaluate ourselves as parents, because we compare ourselves with our own mothers and fathers. We want to do both the good things they did for us and the things we think they should have done for us. We try to avoid the mistakes we judge our parents to have made.

There's nothing particularly wrong with learning from experience and determining to do differently, but it's not what we *do* that spells success or failure, it's the kind of relationship we have with our children. Doing all the right things in the world is not necessarily going to create a good relationship. When we compare ourselves to our folks and then act a certain way with our children because we want to be like—or not like—our parents, we're not being ourselves. We're living in the past, responding to our children as we were, forgetting they are entirely different individuals.

Comparisons with our parents are dangerous for another reason. I may be led to compare my spouse with my mother or father. I may want him to be exactly like—or completely different—than that person. One of the things we need to remember is that our parents weren't always right or always wrong despite what our memory may be of them. Because our memories are slanted, comparisons are unfair. We end up comparing our spouse to a shadow. He has to be allowed to be himself. Every one of us makes mistakes and we do so frequently, but nobody in this world is demanding perfect parenthood. Children are pretty resilient. In terms of not only physical pain but emotional pain. As long as children know they're loved, as long as the children know we're real with them and they can be real with us, they can accept our mistakes. As they recognize our humanity they will more easily recognize their own.

Because we often measure our effectiveness as parents by what our children accomplish, we compare what they're doing with what we did or had to do at a certain age. Does our child ride a bike, play basketball, take care of his room, or help around the kitchen at the same age I did? If he doesn't, we may think we're not as good parents as our parents were. Of course this is nonsense.

We can kid ourselves that we don't compare ourselves with other parents in the neighborhood, but we do. We look at their children's manners, language, cleanliness, neatness, socializing or marks in school. We decide if we're up to snuff, below par, or better than. It's a false standard of comparison. That mentality makes parenthood a performance for the neighbors. It says nothing about the relationship we have with our children.

No one is suggesting that we allow our kids to run wild or ignore the rights of others, but we cannot allow our relationship with them to be determined by our neighbors.

Sometimes we make comparisons between our own children. In almost every family there's an angel and a black sheep. It's easy to think that I'm a good parent in the first case and a bad parent in the second. Neither may be true. I might actually have a very good relationship with the black sheep because he's having a rough time growing up, and a blah relationship with the angel child because he's finding life easy. In any case, the comparison we make is invalid. The best way is to treat each child as custom-made. One child might be outgoing, so he finds it easy to reveal himself, in which case our listening can be more passive. Another might find it more difficult to be open. In that case, we need to create a permissive atmosphere in which that child feels safe with us. One child might have a natural empathy that makes it easy for him to understand what's going on inside us. Another child may seem to never catch on. In that situation we need to take more time and explain our feelings in more detail than we do with the other.

Many of the comparisons we make between children again go back to their performance level. Johnny is doing well in school, Susie isn't; so we think we're a good parent to Johnny and a poor one to Susie. Pam is very obedient, very polite and well-mannered. Billy is noisy, tracks in dirt and doesn't take care of his room. We decide we're successful with Pam and aren't with Billy.

We also use our spouse's parents as a basis for comparison. If they look better than our own parents, we may try to live up to them. We may try to equal them by doing what we think they did. But we can't do the same as they did. Everything is different. And we aren't our spouse's parents.

We can place the external measuring rods of what others think on our spouse, with the same deleterious effects that system of comparisons has on us and our children.

What kind of communication makes a relationship good?   *Your answer:*

In any interaction between persons, there is communication, and it is accomplished by the things we do as well as the words we say. In a family the best communication says, "I love you." By who you are and by what we say and do for our children, we communicate our personal awareness of them, our desire to be closer to them, our eagerness to be present with them and to allow them to be present with us. The little surprises, taking the kids out to the park, playing ball or reading a story to them can be beautiful parts of communication. But sometimes not. We could do them and not have any worthwhile communication in the area of our relationship. When we do something because we think we should—because we want to live up to our responsibilities—whether it's to provide necessary companionship, recreation, consolation or whatever—it usually is empty.

Too often we respond to an obvious external need and don't provide for the internal need. The greatest contribution any mother and father can make to their children is to be present to them. We express it in various ways depending on the child's age, his understanding and his ability to analyze what is happening. With a three-year-old, we might make a fuss over a flower he is squeezing in his hands. With a twelve-year-old, we might praise the first runty little fish he catches. With a sixteen-year old, we might treasure with her the first kiss she's received.

There is difference between spending time doing things for our children and spending time *with* our children. Unless we appreciate occasions for the chance of being with the children, they don't count for much. The reason we care about the things our children

Just being Together is "enjoy"-ment.

do is because we care for *them*. It's more important to be excited about their excitement than to be excited about an occasion. If while we're doing the right thing for our children, we're half-distracted or not with them in spirit as well as in body, we aren't really with them, enjoying them. In later years they'll go off on their own, become interested in doing different things than we do, because we'll have had no common history of enjoying each other over and above whatever we do. Enjoying and appreciating one another regardless of what activity we engage in puts our personal relationship first.

What is the greatest memory you have of being with your children?

Your answer:

We might think of big days like the ones when Cindy learned to ride her bike and Peter finished his first collection for his paper route and when Dad was sick and our little girl Amy sat on the edge of the bed and talked to us. Maybe it was something more—or less—important. But it is not precious because of the event or even the action. It is precious because we shared something of ourselves. It was an occasion when we felt close to our child and he felt close to us. The mutual awareness was precious in itself. What keeps that memory alive is that we experienced each other. There were no barriers between us. We were open to each other. That memory is not dependent upon any particular skills, abilities or education, much less money or social position.

The precious moments between parent and child depend on the interaction of their personhoods. All too often these moments happen almost accidentally. They're here, and then they're gone. They are so beautiful that we should have more of them. A lot of them!

It is a real measure of our success as parents if we are close to our children, so let's consider those moments of magic. Do they touch us frequently? How far back do we have to go to discover a memory like that? Does our child hold that memory as dearly as we do? How many memories does he have of such moments?

How likely is it that something like that could happen tonight? We'd all like to say, "Very likely." If we can't, can we actively determine to create the atmosphere this very day to make another memory come alive? It's so easy to let things go. We can say, "Yes, I know that's the way it should be." Then we get involved in other things or so lack self-confidence that we don't do anything to help it come about.

We can make beautiful moments! They are not something that has to happen by accident. We can create the proper environment by recalling what led to that special memory. What were we doing? What was our son or daughter doing? What were the other members of the family doing? What can we do right now to prepare ourselves to re-create that oneness and openness with our son or daughter? How can we be open and help him to be open and one with us?

A memory that is precious in our lives can be a consolation and an inspiration. It is a gift about which we're wonder-filled. Well then, why restrict ourselves to one memory? Why just hope that maybe it will happen again? Why not determine to make it happen again?

What's the best thing you ever did for your kids?

Your answer:

Well, first and foremost is having them. That may sound like a flip answer, but the truth is we could have chosen not to have them. The gift of life is one that should never be underrated in our hearts or theirs. We are not to use this as emotional blackmail, expecting them to be obedient or to please us because we have graced them with the gift of life. No, that would be wrong. But it's equally wrong to play down the fact that we have given them life. No one else has or can ever do that for them.

There's something deeper too. Not only have we given them life, but that life was given out of our love for each other. It was our desire to respond to each other that caused us to make our relationship permanent by having a child. The life our children have was not an accident of, but a specific expression of what we meant to each other.

We've also given our children their education, good home, food, clothes, medical care and a loving environment. There are many things that could be mentioned, and all of them are fine. But any goodhearted person could provide them.

The unique gift we can continue to give our children is life. It is a fantastic one! It should never be minimized in our hearts or minds. We can listen to them and allow them to listen to us at the level of our real selves. We can communicate in the fullest human sense. Maybe we don't count that because it seems too easy, too cheap; but it actually costs us much more. The price is personal sacrifice. To be real to our children demands the greatest personal self-sacrifice.

If we don't believe that the sharing of ourselves is important, we may try to make up to our children with material things. Then we fall into the trap of "doing" for them, rather than "being present" to them.

The best thing for our kids is ourselves. Cooking and earning a living for them is part of our personhood being spent. There is much more. It is most important for them to get inside of us to see what makes us tick.

We can list all kinds of good things we've done for our children. The sacrifices we've made to drive them to games or parties, the luxuries we have given up so that they could have the right food, clothing and neighborhood. The worry when they were sick or having trouble in school. All these things can come from a sincere heart, but they're inadequate replacements for our personal presence. They enhance, but do not replace listening to our children's real selves and our being open, revealing our true selves.

Pete and Charlotte knew they had a good marriage. They had a great deal in common. Much was already there before they met. When they began dating, they fell in love because they "suited" each other. Their compatibility was an exciting adventure. After they married, their relationship and their family grew. They wanted to pass their life on to the children. They decided to use the family meal. Nothing could be more ordinary; yet it was a very important part of day. Dinnertime was the one time they were all together as a family on a regular basis. They agreed it was to be a fun time and not for preaching or all-out teaching.

Charlotte told Pete, though, that she didn't want the focus entirely on the children. And Pete said he didn't want a "children should be seen but not heard" sort of table. "They're part of the family, too," he told Charlotte.

"That's just what I want them to be, *part* of the family, not *the* family," she said. "I don't want a meal that is totally focused on school, playmates and the latest toy the children want. They need to get their ideas from us, not the other way around. I want them to fit into our conversations, not us into theirs. We can tell them how we feel—honestly—and they can open up to us. Look, Pete, it's the easy way out when we just let them prattle. Then we patronize them or give them advice. When we bring them into our conversations it's much more of an effort because we need to explain more to include them. But that way they learn from us and, besides, their questions make us stop and think."

Pete and Charlotte were actually making it better for the kids, better for then as well as later and laying the basis for adult conversations at the same time.

They also decided that everyone should go to the table as friends. If it was to be a family meal then they wanted to have a family when they sat down. They put their ideas into practice, and the last time they talked to me, everything was going great!

What is the worst thing you ever did to your children?

Your answer:

We are ashamed when we think of the times we haven't paid attention to our children. When we've spent time on ourselves instead of with them, when we've gotten what we wanted instead of what would please them. We have lost our temper, embarrassed them in front of others, let them down.

All these things can have a negative impact on our relationship with our children, but the most devastating practice of all is when we don't allow them inside of us, when we don't let them know who we really are, when we keep ourselves to ourselves. We can spend time with them, try to be responsive to them, and listen with a very sharp ear, but as long as we keep ourselves to ourselves and don't let them see the real human "us," then we can't have a deep relationship with them.

Why don't we reveal ourselves? We're afraid they'll talk to the neighbors or, even worse, to our family. We're fearful that if they know we have doubts and struggles in making decisions, they might use it against us. We're afraid they might take advantage of us. We don't want them to see our weakness, our humanness, our failings. We're fearful they may not pay attention to us if they really know us. But just the opposite can happen. Instead of our kids dealing with us parents with a capital P, they will be responding to warm, loving, human Mom and Dad. Too, it makes it easier for them to talk about their own doubts, worries and concerns.

Which of the previous two questions did you find it easier to answer?   *Your answer:*

Most of us find it easier to answer the last one. We're very aware of our mistakes. They're vivid to us. We either take our good qualities for granted or suppress them because we don't want to seem proud. However, the more we concentrate on our defects, the more likely we are to fall into them. Anybody who always concentrates on how often he strikes out is not going to get ahead, because he's beaten down his self-confidence. A lot of good parents do that to themselves. When they cut themselves down as parents they hurt their kids. This is a self-centered type of mentality. In any human relationship, the more we concentrate on ourselves, the less well we do. When we're absorbed in the other person—the more we concentrate on finding and responding to his goodness—the better we do with that relationship.

We can see this when a boy and girl first meet. Each one is so afraid of doing poorly, so concerned about how he looks, what he's saying and how he's coming across to the other, that both come across as shallow and uninteresting. When we recognize ourselves as good and let the other person loom large in our consciousness, the relationship goes better. We become less self-conscious and more attractive!

If you rate yourself as an average or ordinary parent, what does that do to your children?

Your answer:

If our children's friends told our kids we weren't much, it would upset them. Not just because they love us, but because they'd feel they were being put down. With just plain ordinary parents, how could they be worth very much as persons? So what does it do to our children if *we* say that we're ordinary or average? It makes them feel even less valuable.

It is also true that if we feel we are ordinary, we're bound to treat our children as ordinary. If we rate ourselves as bad or inadequate parents, that's the way we'll rate our children. It's bad enough to put ourselves down, but we have no right to judge ourselves that harshly, because it is a horrible thing to do to our children!

We may say, "Of course I recognize the reality of all this, but I

The hour before Steve dashes off to work is beautiful. We talk about our thoughts and feelings.

honestly am a poor, or at best, an average parent." How did we come to that decision? Is it possible that we compared our child with other children or to our ideal and decided we haven't done well enough? That's a false standard. Besides, our parent effectiveness is not determined by the way the children act. It is determined by how open and responsive the relationship is between us and our children.

It's amazing how our self-confidence will rise once the false measuring sticks are taken away. We can relax and be ourselves.

**Do you expect
yourself to be the
"perfect" parent?**

Your answer:

Most people take parenthood quite seriously and want to do their best. Difficulties come when they can't accept any failure. When we set high standards for ourselves and don't tolerate any mistakes, we're unfair to ourselves and to our children, for no human being can be that perfect. We get uptight and flustered, and the child thinks he's the one to blame for our state.

Furthermore, it's a self-centered approach because we're constantly evaluating ourselves. In always attempting to be right, our focus is on ourselves and rarely on the child. We need to be looking at our children and appreciating each other. We may not be the "perfect" parents, but we'll be a lot closer to it than we think!

**Are you able to
forgive yourself
as a parent?**

Your answer:

Forgiveness is difficult. The old saying goes: "To err is human; to forgive, divine." Everyone finds it difficult to forgive someone who has failed him, someone who has let him down. And yet more often than not we have the courage and generosity to forgive our beloved or our children. The one we find most difficult to forgive is ourself.

We may try to convince ourselves that everything is all right and that we've forgotten our failure, but it often festers within us. We think of our selfishness, our lack of self-control, our jealousy, laziness or whatever defect it was that motivated our poor actions. We can't easily accept the reality of our flawed humanity.

We need to forgive ourselves. If we don't, we aren't accepting the other person's forgiveness, and we can't do that until we have granted it to ourselves.

What are some signs of a poor parent-image?

Your answer:

I may see myself as a poor parent and not realize it. I could even appear to be quite self-confident in that I try to do everything for our children myself. I don't allow my spouse to be involved. That way my mistakes are my mistakes and he doesn't have any right to notice.

On the other hand I could be leaving everything to my spouse. I don't want to get involved. I'm afraid of making mistakes and getting criticized. I let you do everything, so that it's your fault if anything goes wrong.

It's also a sign that I don't think very highly of myself if I'm always critical of what I do. Self-criticism says those things I'm afraid somebody else might say about me. What I say about myself is not so bad as what you say about me. To protect myself, I say it first. Then if you say anything, you're "piling it on."

Our poor self-image shows, too, if we're frequently criticizing the children. And when I say that I'm not much as a parent because I have bratty kids, or if I had better children, I'd do better, I'm blaming them for what I'm considering failure. My own self-rejection is being passed on to them.

A further sign is a dependence on the advice of others. I may constantly read books to find what others have done in my situation, or talk it over with my mother, friends or neighbors. I may seek advice from anyone and everyone to re-enforce a decision. I'm afraid to make a move on my own. If my approach to a situation doesn't work out, then I feel it's not my fault, because I'm doing what those others do or told me to do.

If I mete out severe, lax or inconsistent discipline, I'm probably thinking of myself as a poor parent. Harsh discipline comes from my feeling I'm not good enough to expect the children to do better with reasonable discipline. Lax discipline may be an attempt to get the children to approve of me—because I don't approve of myself.

Do you realize how forgiving your children are?

Your answer:

A magnificent thing about children is how supportive they are of their parents. They search out many excuses to protect them, to explain them. Our children are very generous and loving. They find it easy to forgive us. It is not something of which to take advantage. We should be responsive to their generosity and love, and accept their forgiveness. We hear a lot today about how harshly children, especially adolescent children, judge parents. But we can appreciate how tolerant and eager most young people are to forgive us and begin anew! We shouldn't put a barrier in their way by not forgiving ourselves. When we don't forgive ourselves we can't really accept their forgiveness, and we are less tolerant and forgiving of them.

Why can't you forgive yourself?

Your answer:

Do we actually think we are "perfect" parents, ones who never make a mistake, who always do the "right" thing? No, we know all parents are human beings and make mistakes. Of course, we don't want to make them. We don't want to be "bad" parents. Actually we may take a wrong step very seldom, but if we have a poor parental self-image, it's hard for us to forgive ourselves. As a result, we try to make ourselves worthy. We work hard to live up to an ideal. Naturally we fail, because the ideal is impossible to attain. And the failure re-enforces our low opinion of ourselves as parents.

But we have no right to a poor self-image! It's false and it has a devastating impact on us. It makes our life and that of the children miserable and unhappy. We shouldn't try to impose on them a dream person which no one can live up to!

So one of the first things we have to do for our children's sake is give up the idea that we're poor parents. Holding on to that idea causes us to be so self-involved and so wallowing in self-pity that

We're not ordinary parents — we're special!

we cannot be open to our children either to listen to them or to reveal ourselves. So we have an obligation to change. It is wrong to expose our children to our continuous self-rejection.

What positive steps can you take to think better of yourself as a parent?

Your answer:

The first step in improving our self-image is to determine to start looking at ourselves positively and to eliminate negative criticism and self-rejection. We can stop talking to others about our mistakes. Sometimes we almost brag about how bad we are, about the stupid or mean things we've done, or our careless mistakes.

Complaining to our neighbors about our children being holy terrors or disobedient or lousy students is putting ourselves down indirectly. We expect their "badness" to be our fault, because today it has become commonplace to blame parents for everything their children do. It's not right, but we've become quite conditioned to it. So what begins as criticism of our children becomes self-criticism.

It even happens within the family. We greet our husband with a list of all the wrong things the child did during the day. What we're doing is looking for reassurance. We want to be told that it's not our fault. But we feel bad, because we think we should be able to cope.

Most of all we need to cope with our self-image. Changing to a positive one will only work if we make a real campaign of it. Our poor self-image is such a habit that we have to take drastic steps! We have to be open with our spouse and say, "Look, I'm going to change, but I need your help. Any time I downgrade myself, please hold me or touch me gently and say, 'OK, now say something good about yourself as a parent.'" It's following the law of contraries. Whenever we find ourselves talking negatively about ourselves as parents, then we have to say something we did right or describe some good quality of ours in relationship with the children. In the beginning we may have to force ourselves, but when we make the start, there will be a change.

The next step is to realize how often it is that we are critical of ourselves. A good way to find out is to keep a running record on a piece of paper. Every time we catch ourselves thinking negatively we put a mark down. For every mark on the paper we are to say something positive about ourselves to someone. Does this seem to be opposite from all that we've thought about being modest and not self-centered? Well, we attracted quite a bit of attention with our negative talk! Talking positive may seem senseless. What good will it do? It won't change any actions with the kids. Oh, yes, it will! We will not only feel better about ourselves, but we'll be better with the children. Whenever we're negative about ourselves, we're negative about those around us, so they have a stake in our being positive.

This is not a Pollyanna type of thing. It's real, and it puts our lives as parents in perspective so that we can see that we're good parents. (As long as we think we're bad parents, we're more apt to be just that. And when we do do a good thing, it will be overshadowed by our mistakes and won't have the same effectiveness.

Another step we can take to build our self-image as a parent is to ask our spouse and children to tell the good things they see about us as a father or mother. We have to listen carefully and take on what the other person says. They may say phony things at first, because it's a new type of conversation, but they'll get the idea soon. We'll be surprised and pleased with the good qualities they have seen. Now we won't be so inclined to reject ourselves as parents! Rather, we'll begin to see the good—and accept ourselves.

Does your spouse see himself/herself as a good parent?

Your answer:

You have the best mom in the world — and does she ever love you!

We may feel that because everything seems to go well between our spouse and the children and he or she doesn't complain as much as we do, that his self-image is great. However, our beloved probably feels just about as we do. We could be a part of the other's self-rejection as a parent. We could be contributing to a negative evaluation. Maybe by frequent criticism, by taking over for him, by correcting him in front of the children, or by reversing his decisions, we've taken away his self-confidence.

We may have done this with no ill will. Perhaps we were concentrating so much on the child that we didn't see the effect on our wife or husband. We can help each other to feel otherwise. We need to build up our beloved.

If we have a negative opinion of our spouse as a parent, it's not likely that he has a better one of himself. If we rate our spouse as poor or average, then that's probably how he sees himself. We can help him to see his good qualities as a parent. We can speak frequently about what we find pleasing in him—to him and to others, especially the children. They'll begin to talk positively about how they see him as a parent, and love you both more. Let no opportunity pass to bring out your awareness of the goodness of your beloved as a parent.

What effect do others have on your parent-image?

Your answer:

Without a doubt, the media, the press and general society are eating away at our self-confidence. There's a consensus in our society that parents are the cause of whatever our young people do wrong. All wrongdoing is attributed to the children's upbringing and, specifically, to their parents' relationship with them. Of course parents have a strong influence on their children. However, everyone has a free will, and there are influences other than parents. Parents don't deserve all the blame.

It's hard to shrug off all the propaganda about the failure of parents. The weight of it is tremendous. And because we know we're not perfect, we feel guilty.

In order to counterattack we have to talk to each other positively about what we're doing right, about the good signs of our relationship with our children and the positive effects of our love upon them.

Even more devastating than the media and society can be the impact of criticism from our parents and in-laws. It may be that only one of our parents is hypercritical of one or both of us, but whether it's one or all of them, we have to pull together to overcome this. We have to speak lovingly and honestly to them as we explain what their negativism is doing to us as persons and as parents. They may claim they're saying these things because they love the children and want what's best for them. We must remind them that *we are the best thing for the kids.*

The more we are put down, the more the children are bound to be hurt. No matter what mistakes we make, the worst one is to reject ourselves as parents. This is hard to say to a mother or mother-in-law, but if we believe in each other and care for our children, that's what we have to do. Bitterness or nastiness has no part. If we assume the critical person has good will, we can ask them to be allies in our responsibility to our children. We can explain that we want to be capable of responding to the children properly, but as long as we're being chopped up, we're never psychologically able to respond well. We need them to help by stopping their negative comments. We need them to build us up by recognizing our goodness. If they aren't able to see that we're doing something right, then their view is distorted. We can't always be wrong. The best thing relatives can do for our children is help us to be more aware of our goodness and worth.

No matter how much neighbors may criticize us it won't get to us unless we believe it. We can determine not to allow them to decide what kind of parents we should be.

Because a good husband-and-wife relationship is best for our kids, we have to be united and singleminded in building up each other. When a husband goes on a diet and his wife puts sumptuous meals on the table, they are not of one mind. Neither is a couple of one mind when the wife decides to give up cigarettes and her husband smokes up a storm. Neither the diet nor the giving up of cigarettes will work. When we work together to improve our self-image as parents, we will be successful. A Marriage Encounter couple I know expressed the idea well. Martin said that when he and Jean were covering up their awareness of God's beauty in each other, going in separate directions, the sparks would fly, the smell of sulphur was everywhere—they were split from each other and within themselves. When they were close, trusting, sharing, they were like a team of pretty horses.

How do you feel about teenagers?   *Your answer:*

Today's general attitude toward teenagers is a special problem. We hear negative statements about them practically from the time our children are born. They affect our relationship with our children more than we realize. Someone will tell us, "Enjoy them now, because when they get into their teens, wow!" We're set up to think our children are going to be some kind of monsters when they hit adolescence. We're conditioned to feel that no matter what we do or what relationship we build with our children during the first 13 years of their lives, they're going to become strangers in the house when they hit adolescence. That's almost guaranteeing failure.

Let's not give up that easily. Our children are our children, whether they're 5 or 14 years old, whether they're 16 or 62. The relationship we create in those first years will determine the relationship we have when they're between 13 and 19.

Loving you, it's easy to be a good parent.

The way of expressing our relationship will change through the years. There will be frustrations for us during their teens, but there were frustrations when they were preschoolers! Prejudice against teenagers blocks a good human relationship from developing with them at that stage. We can stop this prejudice by remembering how we felt when we were teenagers and determining to stop criticizing our sons and daughters. Instead we can find their positive aspects. The beautiful things about them. We can talk about these to them, to ourselves and to everyone. Otherwise, we develop a self-fulfilling prophecy. Tell a person often enough that he's a monster, and he'll become one. If we tell our daughter that when she reaches a certain age she'll be impossible to live with, she'll think that's what's expected. She'll give in to her negative feelings and live up to our expectations!

What are the essential qualities of a good parent?

Your answer:

The essential qualities of a good parent are rather simple, nothing fancy, nothing that demands a great deal of education, expertise, insight, incredible energy or great creativity. At the top of the list is listening to our children, listening with the heart and not only the ears.

Next, is responding to them. We need to reach out to them as persons and not just take care of them. We want to allow them to respond, to be fully with us and make their contribution to our lives. They can do more than take little burdens off our back like putting out the garbage, folding the laundry, washing the dishes. They can actually console us, rejoice with us, forgive us.

Another quality of a good parent is the ability to forgive his children. We can do more than just excuse them. We can honestly forgive them and encourage them, rejoicing with them—and enjoying them. One of the greatest gifts we can give our children is to laugh with them. We can take joy in who they are, their simplicity and exuberance, and how good they are.

Every parent reading this is capable of being a better parent. Parents reading this care. They have already put hard work and effort into being good parents. Being a better parent doesn't come automatically. It will be much easier, though, to relate to our children positively if we have a good husband-and-wife relationship. By looking to each other we find our true selves. After all, our parental relationship flows from our marital relationship in more than the physical aspect.

I learned about that when I was visiting friends for dinner. The meal was very pleasant until one of the kids mouthed off to his mother. Immediately tension came into the room. I looked over at the father; he was tight-lipped and red-faced. I thought to myself, "Here it is. I know exactly what's coming. I know what he's going to say." I'd heard the words from my own father and a lot of fathers to their sons. "Don't you dare talk to your mother that way!"

But he didn't say that at all. He said something completely different, and he stopped me just as sharply as he stopped his boy. He said very calmly and very forcefully, "Don't you dare talk to *my wife* that way."

The boy was stunned, and I felt as though I'd just been kicked in the stomach. I saw something I hadn't understood before. I drove home that night, shaken. My face was grey; my hands were knotted around the wheel; my teeth ground together. I felt empty. I was scared and confused. All along I had believed that parenthood was the prime responsibility in marriage. I was helping, guiding, directing, loving young people. That was why I had become a priest. I had built my whole life around helping families, with the emphasis on the kids. I now saw that the real key to kids was *how their parents loved each other.*

I didn't want to pray that night. I knew that it was going to mean a complete change, and I didn't want it. I was 40 years old, really in command of my life, well-trained and doing beautifully, and now I was going to have to start all over again. I was going to have to work with couples. I had to give up those kids of mine—if I really loved them—and work with their parents to make them "couples."

Even worse than the thought of starting again, more painful than the bleakness of being apart from my kids, was what seemed to me to be the hopelessness of it all. People were much more concerned about being "parents" than being "couples." The future seemed to be one of batting my head against a stone wall. Would anyone listen? Yes. Parents are listening. They have a deep underlying hunger to know oneness. As they experience their "coupleness" and keep that first, wonderful things happen in the family.

A very special relationship develops with the children, because then we love them as a part of us, rather than as separate beings. They are an expression of our love for each other. We offer them the unique invitation to continue to "abide in our love." Few children will refuse that offer. And as we recognize the virtues—the good points of our children, we will see our goodness reflected back to us.

The times of laughter are precious. One—
or more — a day will keep the doctor aw

78

Criticism deals with negative
assumptions — not facts.
So, when you open your
mouth to criticize, shut it!

3

CRITICISM

What is the basis for correcting your children?

Your answer:

Our children don't sail on uncharted seas—we've gone through childhood and adolescence and can help them along! That's one of the beautiful things about being parents. We know where many choices will lead, so we can help our children make better choices than they could make by themselves. Being aware that certain steps are necessary in order to develop habits and qualities that are essential for successful living, we can guide our children.

When we are young we are apt to live for the moment. We respond to whatever attracts us or avoid whatever seems unappealing. As we mature, we become more capable of making immediate sacrifices for long-term goals. Although this is hard for youngsters to see, it's essential for them to learn to say yes sometimes when they want to say no, and no sometimes when they want to say yes. That's where parents come in. The man and woman children call father and mother have gone through such times. They have experienced the disaster of sacrificing a greater good for immediate satisfaction. They have learned the value of postponing and preparing.

Our children are not bad, they just haven't formed their values yet. Parents aren't supposed to make all the decisions for their children, but they can help provide what may be lacking in the child's judgment, maturity, experience or establishment of his goals.

Anyone who is not experienced tends to be unsure, tentative, blundering. This is understandable. Well, our children are novices at life. They're unsure about themselves, their abilities and their potentials. They're tentative about other people and their relationships with them. They're blundering in things they say and do. It's all new to them, so we can't expect them to be smooth and professional.

It is a great gift from parents to their children to point out with gentleness and love the long-term consequences of activities or decisions. We can show them the effects on others of things they say or do. We can help them see that the talents they apply in limited areas have broader dimensions. We can help and encourage them not to give up when things don't work out for them immediately.

Another gift parents can give their children is help in the decision-making process. We can help them gather information, weigh it and take note of its most important elements. We can look together at the various decisions that could be made and consider the possible consequences of the various ones. We can consider with the child how each decision affects him, how each affects others, especially those close to him. We can point out the hidden dimensions of a decision. We have learned that when we make some choices, they preclude decisions on things we haven't thought of. For instance, having a puppy at Grandma's in the summer is fine, but it's a whole new situation at home in the 5th floor apartment in the winter. We parents can also help our children to see that making a decision is only half the battle. To be worth anything it has to be carried out and carried out well.

Some of the greatest graces given parents are those of guiding, directing, correcting and informing the children. This is the most important process of their education. The schools are concerned with the discipline of learning—to teach children to use their intellectual faculties. The real education—derived from the Latin word *educere*, meaning to draw out of—happens in the home. With parents guiding, giving direction and pointing the way, the child does not flounder and get lost. He has a guiding star.

Most parents understand the responsibility of guidance and direction and take it on very well. They see the necessity of it and sincerely try to assist their children.

When does your correction become criticism?

Your answer:

Centuries ago sailors thought the earth was flat because it seemed that the sea stretched out before them on one plane. They drew a wrong conclusion because they didn't have the right perspective. Our children can draw wrong conclusions in the decisions they make, the activities they engage in, or the type of friends they choose, because they lack the necessary perspective. Today we wouldn't let someone who believed the earth is flat be a navigator. That would lead to disaster. So we have not only a right, but an obligation to correct our children. They need to recognize their mistakes.

It's one thing to correct our children. Correction is objective. Correction only points out the truth or falseness of an action, a statement, a choice or habit. Criticism is quite different. It goes on to ascribe a negative personal motivation to the action. It attacks the person. It inflicts a personal judgment. It's one thing to say,

"Two plus two does not equal five, Billy. It equals four." That is correction. It's something else if you add, "You're so careless!" Using the the word *careless*—or a tone of voice that implies it—transforms the legitimate correction into criticism! And criticism is devastating if it's done frequently and in a number of areas.

Some of us become convinced that if we can point out a personal failing behind a mistake (that's criticism) then our correction will be more powerful. No, it won't be. Instead we take away a person's self-respect. If we parents, the most important people in our children's lives, don't respect them, how can they respect themselves?

Our criticism often stems from our own self-criticism. We are too quick to identify our own or our spouse's failings—laziness, coldness, carelessness, insensitivity or whatever—as personal failings in the child when they may not be present at all.

We know from our experience that it's hard enough when someone points out a mistake we've made, but if we're told we made the mistake because of deficiencies in our character then it's much harder. It can even cause a break in the relationship. If a husband says to his wife, "You're not listening to me," that's one thing. If he says, "You're not listening to me—because you don't ever care about me," that's quite different. In the first instance the wife can admit she wasn't listening. She's human and even in the closest love relationship we don't listen at times. In the second instance, if she admits she wasn't listening she's saying—from her husband's point of view—that she doesn't care. That isn't fair—or right!

It's perfectly legitimate to say to our children, "This homework is not done well. The answers are incorrect." But it's not fair to say, "This homework looks as though it were done by an idiot," or, "You never try, do you?" The criticizing puts the child on the defensive. With the correction, the child may feel bad that he didn't do a good job, but he won't feel put down as a person. If he has to admit he's an idiot or doesn't try, that's much more serious. To point out to child that he wasn't home on time and dinner had to be postponed is a needed correction. However, if we add that he did it because he is thoughtless and careless, then we're engaging in criticism. We're on a personal level where feelings are hurt and both sides get defensive. It isn't good or wise to do that. We don't even have the right to do it. For how can we be certain

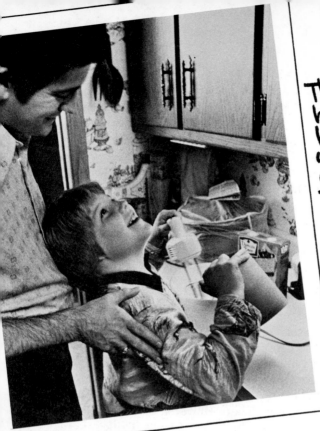

This will be the best cake you've ever tasted!

that the motivations we ascribe to our children are accurate? Teachers have had experiences where they were convinced a child was inattentive and unconcerned, and it turned out that the child had trouble hearing or seeing. Or a child was defiant or bored in the classroom and it wasn't because he was "bad." He was bright and far ahead of the others.

Even around the house we often tag our kids, thinking we know exactly what personal failings are behind the mistakes they make. Maybe we ought to pay attention to the evidence that contradicts what we think. Take the child who never helps around the house. Is it because he's lazy? Or might it be because he doesn't have a sense of personal responsibility?

One of the most exciting experiences for a child is to be allowed to stir up something in the kitchen. His face lights up when he approaches making a cake or brownies. Why? Because he knows he's doing something creative and making a real contribution. People are going to be pleased and he's going to get the credit.

The problem with daily chores is that there's little credit involved. The first few times the child does his job he likes doing it. There's some credit, and doing the work is a sign he's growing up. But after a while he stops because nobody notices; his job no longer seems to be a contribution. He's low man on the totem pole. So he ducks out whenever he can. The cause is not a character defect. On the parent's side, the child looks lazy and uncooperative. On the child's side, the parents are giving the dirty jobs to the kids. Result: a personal confrontation.

All of us find it fairly easy to accept correction, especially if it's done gently and lovingly. We recognize when we make mistakes. But we find it difficult to take criticism even if it's offered gently and from the best motives. Knowing that, we shouldn't put our children in the position of being criticized. It isn't necessary and it doesn't work. So the guidance and direction we offer should be without criticism.

There's another problem with our criticizing. It leads to counter-criticism. The children learn from us—at a very early age—to criticize. Imitating us they return our criticism. They may not do it to our faces, because then we'd criticize them for that, but they do it within their hearts. However, they feel quite free to be critical of one another and their friends. Criticism creates an atmosphere of fear and distrust, the exact opposite of the atmosphere we want for family living. If a child knows that not only his actions are going to be judged, but he is, he'll be uptight, cautious and protective. He can't be open and fully receptive to a warm relationship in the family. That is a devastating situation.

Criticism actually amounts to character assassination. If a child hears often enough that he's selfish and unmindful of others, he begins to believe it. Soon he stops making efforts to be thoughtful of people, because it's not expected from him. He's been told this is not one of his characteristics. He becomes more selfish. If children are told often enough that they're not to be trusted with practical things, then gradually they fit into that mold. A child who isn't to wash the dishes because he always breaks something, one who can't go to the store because he'll get lost, get the wrong can or drop the bag, won't be very eager to help with chores.

Probably the worst result of criticism is that we lose reverence for one another. Criticism damages the personhood of the individual involved. As the criticizer, we're saying the other person is deficient. We're also showing our lack of respect for him. We're both hurt.

Many good mothers and fathers worry about losing their tempers with their children, not paying enough attention to them, giving them too harsh punishment or being too lax. They go around in circles trying to live up to the responsibilities God has given them as parents. They analyze, discuss and read books to learn how to be better parents. But no matter how much they try to correct their relationship with their children, if the frequency and intensity of the criticism doesn't change, they haven't improved very much. The basis for good family relationships is reverence for one another. Criticism is a cancer that eats away that reverence. It's a malignancy in the love relationship between parents and children.

Why do parents criticize?

Your answer:

Our impulse to criticize comes initally from our love and concern for our children. We want what is best for them. We want to protect them from mistakes that could impair their happiness.

There isn't a parent in the world who doesn't want a great future for his children. And parents are very conscious of the mistakes they made growing up. Many still affect them. Knowing the pain and disappointment involved, they want to prevent the same thing from happening to their children.

We tend to be very careful with anything that is important to us. We cherish an old snapshot that is the only picture of our mother and father together. We don't leave it lying around. If we buy a new car, we treat it very well. We like the new car smell. It's not just a car, it's new and we don't want it to get a dent or a scratch.

The same is true with our children. They're precious to us and we do everything we can to be sure they're protected. We constantly plan how we can do more for them, what opportunities we can offer them, what hardships we can spare them. We may have even come to the point of knowing that a person is his own worst enemy, and that each of our children has himself to contend with. They have to learn to make decisions, provide for themselves and others. They each are to make a contribution to this world with his talents and abilities. We know that unless they have internal strength and security, an ability to be honest with themselves and a consistency in searching out their goals, their lives won't be very pleasant.

As a result, we point out where they're failing, not from hostility, not to pick on them, but because we love them. In doing so, no matter how deep our love, we miss the major purpose of what parent and children are all about. It's understandable. Criticizing is deeply ingrained in us. Our parents criticized us. It seemed to be a part of parenthood. Even if we didn't like it! We loved our parents, and they employed criticism, so it seemed to be a necessary requirement.

Parental authority plays a large part in our criticizing. In suspecting that our kids may pull the wool over our eyes we jump on them with negative comments. We don't want them to consider us naive or unaware. If they did, we think we'd lose their respect. So we create circumstances in which the children lose respect for themselves! By criticizing we remove their self-appreciation. And we don't succeed in maintaining their respect, because as their self-rejection increases so does their rejection of us.

Much of our need to criticize, of course, comes from our own self-rejection. We possess traits that we don't appreciate. We see our failings and we don't like ourselves very much. Those traits seem to have held us back in life or kept people from liking us. When we recognize these in our children, we instinctively lash out. We don't want them to be like us in those respects. We want to change them.

My friend Martin described when he was most apt to criticize. "I get wrapped up in my wordly affairs and cultural practices and forget that each member of our family is one of God's beautiful creations. Then I tear apart, chew out, pick on, snap at, and fight myself and my family. My feelings are like those of a kitten cornered under a chair by a dog. I spit and scratch and my hair stands on end. I criticize everybody for everything.

"When I accept God in me, I accept him in my family. Then it feels like a shower has just passed and we are under a beautiful rainbow. I find patience, warmth, strength and security. At times like these I seem to have an uncanny ability to figure things out and to help the children—without criticizing."

Our criticism is also influenced by the attitude that society has toward children and young people. Any time our children's behavior comes close to resembling publicized trends that we don't like, we include our children in the negative picture that has been painted for us.

Sometimes we may criticize our children because we are being criticized for their conduct. We're embarrassed by what other people think of us. Those other people may even be our own parents.

What is the effect of your parents' criticism on you?

Your answer:

The criticism we received when we were growing up is still with us. Whether our parents criticized us often or seldom, it has made us less free to be ourselves. Criticism teaches us to be self-analytical and cautious. A bit is not harmful, but large, regular doses destroy us. We talk about not sticking our necks out. The implication is that we'll get our heads chopped off if we do. The deepest and most serious effect of criticism is that it reduces the way we exercise our capabilities. We are hesitant to get involved in anything unless we know we'll be successful and accepted.

For instance, if we are told during our formative years that we have no staying power and that we're wishy-wasy, then we're going to find it hard to seriously consider getting involved in anything that calls for consistency or long-term commitment no

Seeing the best in each other makes a difference.

matter how much we are convinced of its value. Years ago we were persuaded that we don't have the capability.

Or we may have been told again and again that we were selfish and insensitive to people. Gradually the drip, drip, starts to eat away at us and we accept selfishness and insensitivity as part of who we are. Ultimately we don't even try. After all, it's easier to let others exercise sensitivity.

Criticism bites deeply into many other good qualities, including patience, intelligence, good judgment. It's frightening. It creates a prison for our soul. Our body may be free, we may be able to walk anywhere on the face of the earth, but in our thinking we're limited in what we should try.

These days we're beginning to see what has happened to women over the centuries, how their full human potential was diminished by society's expectations for femininity. Aggressiveness in women was criticized. We now see the quality as initiative and appreciate it. The strength to stand by convictions and the ability to make decisions were labeled a negative "dominance" if possessed by a female!

We did the same thing in regard to men. Because we equated gentleness with weakness, we labeled a boy feminine when we were aware that he was a feeling person and began to deprive him of his capability for sensitive personal relationships.

After a while a criticism doesn't have to be imposed. It's been heard so much that it's become a part of the person. A girl's parents wouldn't even have to tell her anymore that she's domineering and aggressive or plain and awkward. She tells herself. A boy doesn't have to be told that having feelings is a sign of weakness. He knows it well and makes sure his feelings don't show. Oh yes, we can be certain that our parents' criticism of us worked. It is evident in the way we see ourselves and the way we live today.

In our adult life we want to think we've overcome the criticism we've received. We think we have enough security and ego strength to disregard its effect. But it still determines how we relate to the members of our own family, what we look for in them, what we expect from them. It's important to look back over our early years to find out what criticisms were most frequent and hurtful. We don't do this to put down our parents. We do it to counteract their present effect on our lives from way back then.

A doctor usually asks if we've had previous diseases. It enables him to diagnose the present in view of the past and then prescribe the right treatment. Once we identify the criticisms in our past and determine which negative characteristics were ascribed to us, we can recognize where we are at the present. Then we can learn how to overcome some of our personal deficiencies.

Maybe our fear of speaking up makes us keep quiet about our ideas, and our boss thinks we have nothing to contribute. On the other hand, we may overcompensate. A boy accused of being namby-pamby may develop all the classic patterns of masculinity and a girl whose femininity was questioned may become an active Women's Liberationist.

Another effect of the criticism we've received all our lives is that we mistake correction for criticism. When somebody simply points out a mistake we've made, no matter how objectively, we still hear personal criticism behind the words! If we won't—or can't—realize the difference, we might be inclined to react in one of two ways. We might become the touchy type of person and not work well with others—or we might become a passive personality and look for and expect criticism around every corner. Neither is desirable.

We are not compelled to continue to accept all that past criticism for ourselves or to keep on inflicting it on our children. We can change. Our happiness is at stake and that of the people around us. All of those with whom we have relationships are dependent on our awareness of our value and worth and theirs. We can break the chain of criticism from generation to generation by breaking with the negatives of our past and by not criticizing our children.

Do you criticize your children equally?

Your answer:

In all probability we do not criticize our children equally. We mean to be fair, but it could be that we're more demanding of our oldest than of our youngest. Or we're looking for all our children to live up to the child who is the most talented, most docile or most helpful. Maybe our different ways of criticizing or its frequency are determined by sex. Or, because the personalities of the children vary, our criticism may be determined by the degree of compatibility we experience with each one.

External influences also play a role in the way we treat each of our children. If we live in a neighborhood of older people who are bothered by youngsters, our most active child will likely be the most scolded. If there is a lot of tension involved in our work or if our marital relationship is under pressure, the children will seem to be more of a burden. The one who makes a fuss or gets in our way increases our frustration and gets the criticism whether he deserves it or not!

It's safe to say, too, that the intensity of our criticism varies from child to child. It's helpful to figure out which of our children gets the heaviest doses of criticism and which one gets the lightest. Sometimes we get into a pattern without being aware of what we're doing, so that just recognizing the pattern is a big step toward a cure. Then we need to find the cause for the pattern.

We need to look at the differences in the children. The one who experiences the most criticism is certainly the most tense whether he shows it or not. (Don't mistake withdrawal for freedom from anxiety. A lonely child is under a great deal of inner tension.) The one who receives the most criticism usually dishes it out to his siblings and peers and is critical of his teachers and any other adults with whom he is in contact. The teacher—no matter how good—may be the lightning rod to drain off the hostility and resentment the child has toward us.

The heavily-criticized child is liable to be a perfectionist. He feels compelled to do everything just right. He's never satisfied with his performance. Constantly he's either trying to achieve or, on the other hand, he gives up and finds it difficult to take any initiative. Because he is more aware of his capacity to fail than of his capacity to succeed, he is often timid.

The heavily-criticized child has difficulty relating to his brothers and sisters and his peer group. He has a tendency to be a loner. He may be bossy and go out of his way to form associations with others in the same boat. Criticism has usually convinced the problem children in a class or neighborhood that they are considered to be failures. They form their own subculture where the rules are different and they can be successes.

The least criticized children in the family are most able to be themselves. Not always having to be right, they have less pressure; they are the least uptight. They can make mistakes without being jumped on. There is more joy and fullness in their lives.

What is the connection between your criticism of the children and your relationship with your spouse?   *Your answer:*

Because we think of ourselves as intelligent and fair human beings, we think we can keep relationships separate. We don't want to see that when our relationship with our husband or wife is going badly that it affects how we criticize our children. But it does.

Our present relationship with our children is largely determined by what our relationship is with our spouse. Rather than being dismayed, we can realize the other side, too. When we're appreciating each other, a lot of love and sincere thoughtfulness spills over onto our children. We see them in light of the way we're seeing our husband or wife. Because children are an expression of our relationship, not only physically, but in their total personal being, when we're criticizing our children, we're criticizing ourselves and our mates!

We have to look for the source of our criticism. Why are we so sharply critical of our spouse? What has to change in our marital relationship to be rid of our critical spirit? (There's a whole Evening on this in "More Evenings for Couples.")

One obvious source of our criticism is due to characteristics we ascribe to men or women. But we're in for a change. We're actually living in two worlds. We're being freed from the one where men and women have their prescribed roles to the one where everybody can be a full-fledged person in every aspect. During this generation we can grow in responsiveness as never before, because we are encouraged to be ourselves.

However, we will still criticize our children, sending signals about what we like and don't like about our spouse—even though it won't be on a sexist basis—if we don't do something about our basic attitudes. There are better ways to correct our beloved than to criticize our children.!

How do your expectations affect your criticism?

Your answer:

Our expectations for our children loom large in our consciousness and deeply affect our whole relationship, including criticism. We hold our children up against our ideal image and want them to conform. When they can't, we often criticize. It is a major way to try to enforce our expectations.

Our expectations don't come out of thin air. They come from our self-image, most especially where we consider ourselves to be lacking. They còme from the way we see our parents and our spouse. Looking at them we discover clues as to where we are in relationship with ourselves and our husband or wife and our children. They give us tips on changes we have to make in ourselves and our relationships.

Many times our expectations for our children are not fundamentally our own. We may have adopted those of our parents or our spouse's parents. We need to rethink where we are. We also need to consider what expectations we have concerning our spouse as a parent and how they influence our criticism.

A husband and wife have definite expectations of each other as father and mother. If the way the children act makes the husband look bad as a parent in his wife's eyes, he's going to be tempted to put the blame on the children and criticize them plenty. Talking over our feelings will bring to light why we criticize the children the way we do. There are probably all kinds of assumptions. Finding out what's behind our negative attitudes, clarifying our expectations, even wanting to eliminate them, puts us ahead of where we are now. And there's some distance to go before we can get on top of the situation. All the resolutions in the world to stop criticizing the children will fail until we attack the source, which is our expectations of each other as parents. So, we need to take the first step and identify them.

It's easy to defend our expectations as reasonable or good. But whether they are or not isn't the point. The crux of the matter is that our expectations are a control on our husband or wife. By our expectations we are trying to force the person to become the kind of parent we want him to be. And because our expectations are so engrained in us, we pursue them, wanting them in our spouse without realizing it.

When he doesn't live up to our expectations, we're dissatisfied. We tend to criticize him and try to compensate for his "deficiencies." The effect on our sons and daughters is that we undercut

I don't want anything to change here.
I love you, our kids and our meals!

their relationship with that parent. Subtly we cause them to be dissatisfied with him or her.

Once we admit our expectations and come to an honest realization that we have to allow our spouse the freedom to be himself with the children, then the two of us can work together. When we can take pleasure in each other and our relationships with the children without putting our own demands on each other, our tendency to be critical with the children will disappear. The more we learn to grant freedom to each other, be lovingly responsive to each other and to celebrate the other's qualities and gifts, the more we'll be able to be that way with our children. Once we stop looking for our spouse to live up to our idealistic expectations, we'll take the pressure off our children to live up to the idealistic expectations we have for them.

What is "constructive" about constructive criticism?   *Your answer:*

We may think we can put our criticism in the category of being "constructive" because we feel our motives are good. After all, we want what's best for the child and offer "constructive" criticism to help. But, actually, that doesn't change it's thrust. We may be as objective in our comments as possible. We may not engage in angry attempts to demean our child. Our words may be temperate. But if we assign motives, any motives at all, that's personal. And there is nothing more personal than a person's shortcomings. Billy doesn't like to be told that he tore his jeans because he is thoughtless and wants to make more work for his mother. Jeanie is rather mystified about being asked hysterically why she was trying to kill herself when she was riding her bike down the driveway.

If an adult gets uptight with our criticism we sometimes excuse ourselves by saying, "Don't take it so personally. I was only trying to help." If our child gets more upset that we expected, we are ashamed and his hurt becomes ours.

When we give "constructive" criticism we believe that our goal is to help build the child. But we are actually tearing him down. We're talking about his personal defects. We're destroying him. That's ironical, isn't it? Nothing is constructive about criticism. Nothing at all. Criticism ascribes negative motivation to whatever the child did or didn't do, and that is always destructive. It is correction that can be constructive, because it's concerned with the accuracy of an action, a statement or a position.

When we offer correction—real help—we don't focus on the shortcomings, we give guidance, and we direct, encourage and support the child. Correction points out what is incorrect about what the child did or didn't do. It doesn't tell him he tried to be mean or careless or whatever. Maybe something said had a bad effect or an omission left someone with more work. In correction we assume that the motivation of the other person is good. Even as we point out the wrong action and its effects we imply the goodness of the person we're correcting. Supplying bits of information to give understanding in the situation and to prevent a recurrence of the unfortunate word or action is the type of thing that is helpful and generally appreciated.

With criticism we assume ill of the other person. We imply that he knew of the bad effect ahead of time and either didn't care or, if he did care, he didn't care enough to change. We may even imply there's something wrong with the person because he didn't anticipate the results of what he did. It's difficult to see how this can be considered constructive.

Whenever we need to correct a child and we begin to slip over into criticism we need to consider the effect on the child. Criticism, since it is personal and negative, takes away the child's self-confidence and self-appreciation. Because we don't want that to happen, we better stay on this side and keep with correction. We better learn how not to criticize! We'll all be happier.

Do you automatically assign negative characteristics to each child?

Your answer:

I know they didn't try to be late for supper.
Why did I criticize and make a big deal of it?

It's always a temptation for parents to assign certain negative characteristics to each child. One is slow, another is our cry-baby, one is oversensitive, another is awkward, one is a terror. Almost always comparisons are involved. We compare our children to one another or to what we expect of each child. Lorraine is careless, Bobby is neat. Bettie is a mumbler. Comparisons and characteristics are odious. They don't let the child be himself. The labels become set before a child is four or five and it's practically impossible for him to dig his way out. Even when he tries to be different, we're surprised, because we've already determined what he's like. The negative characterization becomes a self-fulfilling prophecy. Try as he might, the child can't get rid of the tag we've placed on him.

It's possible that the negative characteristics we assign to our children are what we inadvertently expect from them. For example, in comparison with our girls we label our boys as untidy or unaffectionate. We may complain but at the same time we say to ourselves, "That's the way boys are." The message comes across that boys are supposed to be rough, track in mud, and leave the table cluttered. When we begin to see what characteristics we are applying to our children, we need to discover the part we're playing in making them that way.

Negative labeling is frequently done by good mothers and fathers along with a tolerant smile or a little joke. Sometimes comments are made about how we're all human and aren't perfect. We forget what that type of thing did to us. If we think back, we can remember times when we tried desperately not to be known as lazy or slow or whatever, and how we couldn't get away from that family opinion. We need to consider how nice it would be to not have labels and pigeon holes for everyone. It would be a release, something worth trying!

Do you have a critical nickname for each child?

Your answer:

We all know how much our names mean to us. We're careful with our names, and we want to be called the name that pleases us most. We particularly care about the affectionate diminutives or fun nicknames that are special or intimate.

Most parents have spent a lot of time and effort to select the right name for each child. Before the child is born, names are discussed in connection with relatives and friends and famous people, and said over and over to feel the sounds. Part of choosing a name carefully is that each name indicates a certain personality type, a certain list of qualities (which may be different for various people). Nonetheless that's one reason why a lot of parents don't like nicknames for their children.

Then why do *we* spoil all that by giving our children negative nicknames? "Oh, I mistook you, you're not William, you're Lazy Bones." "You're not Maureen, you're Slowpoke." We give names to our children which tell them and everyone around what we think of them.

At times we do this half in jest. But that's the point. Half is not in jest! A child doesn't know whether to laugh or cry. We're giving him a name that sums up our opinion of him. It is insulting and it hurts. We might call the slow poke "Greased Lightning," or the

We will pick a name that will be as beautiful as our baby ...

one with the questioning mind, "Mr. District Attorney." There are other common nicknames like Prima Donna, Lazy Bones, Tattle Tale, Bully, Miss Prim, or Sloppy Joe. The point is that the nickname ascribes a negative characteristic to the child. It probably brings laughter and jibes from the other children, making it even harder to take. We express our disappointment or disapproval of our child every time we call him that name. After a while the name seems natural to us and maybe even to the child, but the damage is done. Try the opposite sometime! Great things can be accomplished with complimentary nicknames. A girl glows when she hears herself greeted with "Hi, Beautiful" or "Hello, Princess." In that regard I can still remember all the details of something that happened 33 years ago.

Geometry was the third class of the day. I was sitting in the middle row, second seat from the back. I was 5'2", 100 pounds. It seemed everybody was bigger than I was. Besides, I was a mama's boy and didn't have many friends. Tony LaBeau, who was teaching the class, was writing on the left-hand side of the blackboard and asking us questions. He looked at me and called on me. He said, "Chuck—" That was the first time in my life I had ever been called Chuck. Up until then I had always been "Charles." A thrill shot through me. I knew what he was doing. I wasn't very insightful or sharp, but I knew what he was doing! He was giving me my manhood! I wasn't a little kid any more with a squeaky, little voice. I was *Chuck!* Maybe I still didn't look very big, but Chuck was a man's name—it had size to it.

I guess, in a way, Tony is my father. He gave me my name. I've never failed to pray for him every day since for being so sensitive, so noticing of this garmy little kid. I've never been the same since. That name gives me confidence and strength to this day. As "Chuck," I feel power and life coursing through my veins. Our names are symbols of how we see ourselves and how others see us.

Do you speak critically of your children to others?

Your answer:

Our generation has developed the habit of being "open and frank" about almost everything, including our children. There's something cynical about it. We don't want to be accused of being doting parents, so we talk openly about the negative aspects of our children and our relationship with them. We don't want to be looked on as naive, so we show that we can criticize our children with the most sophisticated eye.

In past generations people played oneupmanship with their friends about their children—how good they were and what good marks they got—anything and everything of which parents were proud was discussed. Now we play "Can You Top This?" with the negatives. We sing the "Nobody knows the troubles I've seen" refrain to our friends. "You think your kids are bad—wait till you hear about mine."

We seem to do this even with our parents and brothers and sisters. We build prejudice in grandparents and aunts and uncles against our children! Imagine that! There should be intimacy and privacy within our home. We know how we resented our parents telling others about our bad points or talking about things we wanted kept secret. And we don't appreciate our children telling others when we lose our tempers or forget something important.

It is true that sometimes we want and need advice on how to handle a problem, so we discuss it with someone outside the family. That's not the same thing. When we really want help we choose our counselor carefully and make sure the child is not hurt. A child feels terrible when he knows we are talking about him to others. If we could understand that, maybe we would do it less.

A prime concern in any home is the kind of relationship and communication that exists between members of the family. Trust is an important aspect of good communication, and our children sense a violation of trust when we talk about their shortcomings to relatives and friends. The problem becomes compounded inasmuch as our children then don't trust us in other areas. We can forgive ourselves on the basis that being critical of our children to others is not as serious a violation as it would be if they were adults. "They're only children." Only! It's the most important time of their lives! What's done now is done. We shouldn't have a double standard—one set of rules for our children and another set for ourselves—especially when we've mixed up our priorities. It's our children who are most important!

We can learn to keep our mouths shut and not pass on to others our criticisms of our children. We may not even be right! Some people think that when they are critical they are being honest. But our opinions don't make something true; they only express our feelings. We'd probably be more accurate to tell people how good our children are than to tell how bad they are. There's far more goodness than badness in our children to talk about! It's bad enough when we criticize our sons and daughters to themselves. We compound the felony when we discuss it with other people. We'd be amazed at how far this gossip, and gossip is the word for it, spreads. Our children get known among all our relatives and neighbors, their classmates and teachers, as having certain negative characteristics. If other people are going to become aware of our children's defects, let them do it on their own. Let's not do it for them. We need to exercise a bit of discipline on ourselves. Then we'll establish a strong basis for an atmosphere of trust and confidence between ourselves and our children.

Are your children more aware of your approval or your disapproval?

Your answer:

If we asked our children to describe what we like and dislike about them, what would they say? Have we made them more conscious of their good points or their bad points? Unfortunately, they are usually more conscious of their bad points.

Why? The difficulty begins with the way we look at parenting. We are apt to take the view that as parents it's our job to accomplish certain goals with our child by the time he graduates from high school. As he grows up we keep looking for what still has to be done. We don't at any time see the job as finished. Yes, he learned to read. And yes, he pretty much keeps his room in order.

But we still have to work on the bad points. He doesn't always get his reports in on time. He doesn't always practice as much as we think he should—or remember to talk to Grandpa. As the child gets older we see we have less and less time to achieve our goals, so we concentrate even more on the bad points. Our natural tendency is to be conscious of what's lacking! What is good we don't have to worry about, consequently we don't give it much attention!

Therefore, our children feel that we are more conscious of where they are weak than of where they are strong. They have little doubt but that we are displeased with certain aspects of who they are. This realization is a big thing in their relationship with us.

The child's awareness of our disapproval leads to a distance between us. We have destroyed the very thing that is the main goal of parenthood, which is to build a love relationship between parents and children. We know it's very difficult to be close to someone if we sense their disapproval, so why have we done it? Can we change our focus? Approval supports and encourages all the essential areas of a love relationship: communication, trust, listening, forgiveness, healing. When disapproval is present in a relationship, we tend to concentrate on the cause of that disapproval rather than on each other. Our relationship takes second place.

In most cases criticism is unfair and when unfairness exists it makes it difficult for our children to respond to us. Fairness is a tremendously important quality in our children's eyes. Even when being fair hurts them, they respect us for it. Criticism is unfair because it always highlights what we disapprove of. It wipes out the overall good. It's as if we had a magnificent diamond with a tiny flaw and instead of looking at its beauty we took a magnifying glass and studied the flaw. We spoil our enjoyment of the gem. Our critical spirit is the magnifying glass we use on our children. We miss their beauty by focusing on their shortcomings.

I had that experience with adults on a Marriage Encounter Weekend. I was ready to give the first talk and a couple came in. They were ugly! Both of them! He was fat, had a lot of frizzy hair and a bulbous nose. She was dumpy and pock-marked. But worse then that, their eyes and their mouths were ugly too. His were blank and staring. Hers were sharp and hostile, with lips tightly

drawn and pursed. I had an instant revulsion to them. I didn't even want to look at them. So, what did they do? They plunked themselves down in the front row. They took those seats all weekend long. I kept saying all the right words during that Encounter—love each other, listen to each other, be pleased with each other, delight in each other. But with them sitting there right

You kids sure put together an original letter To Uncle George. He'll want to stay in the hospital!

in front of me I found it hard to get the words out. How could I ever ask him to tell her she was beautiful? And there was nothing nice looking about him that she could tell him about.

But Sunday morning came and they were shining! They were easily the best-looking couple in the room. I couldn't believe it. They hadn't lost any weight, his hair wasn't any different, and she still had her pock marks. But they were gorgeous! Their faces radiated, their smiles glowed and their eyes gleamed. It was a miracle. They told us what had happened.

She said, "Last night for the first time in 22 years my husband told me that I was beautiful—and I know he meant it. It was in his eyes."

He said, "I'm the luckiest man in the world. She loves me! She said so last night without my asking."

I had never believed in fairy stories, but if ever a frog had turned into a prince—if ever there was a Cinderella who threw away her rags—this was it.

... I like to look on myself as one who faces blunt reality. I'm not a dreamer. I take things as they are. I can't stand people who kid themselves. I keep my feet firmly planted on the ground and base my reactions to life on the way things are, not on the way I'd like them to be. I never wish upon a star or throw three coins into a fountain. So after my first stunned reaction, after celebrating that couple's joy, after being wonder-filled about the change in them, I had some unfinished business. Me! And what my thoughts about their ugliness on Friday night said about me. Now I was ugly. I felt slimy, crawly, with rough scales all over me. I wanted to disappear, I didn't want to be near anyone. I figured it had to show on my face. I didn't want anybody to touch me. I must be contagious.

Their beauty had been there all along. It had been shining inside them just waiting to be recognized. Because of my interior ugliness, I had never even looked. I hadn't even thought of looking. What was worse, I had been convinced there was nothing to find. I always prided myself on being like the boy who recognized that the Emperor had no clothes. Then, like a laser beam, the recognition sliced into me. I was one of those who was fooled by appearances. All I saw was how they looked. I didn't see *them*. I shrank from myself. Now I was even more bothered. Was I going to see the next ugly man as a frog instead of a prince? The next unattractive woman's rags instead of her beauty? I was so good at being a realist! How was I ever going to change? After all, you might find one prince, but frogs are frogs, right? Suddenly it struck me. I wasn't that "feet-on-the-ground" type of person at all. It was I who had been living in a dream world. Frogs only exist in fairy tales. In real life there are only princes.

Could your children write down what displeases you about them?

Your answer:

Each of our children know what they get scolded for. They are very aware of where they fall down in our eyes. They could probably fill up a sheet of paper, writing down the defects we have revealed to them about themselves. Could they do the same thing writing down what we praise them for? Probably not.

This comes from the perfectionism we teach our children. It's easier for them to think about their defects, because that's what we're always talking about. Let's consider impatience. They would list it because they sometimes lose their tempers. Because they sometimes lose their tempers they don't think of themselves as patient. They would never write that down. The child considers impatience as a flaw if it's ever present in his personality. But patience, the virtue, doesn't count unless it's *always* present. We teach our children a double standard!

Here's an example. We complain about children's athletic leagues, particularly the way coaches deal with the youngsters on the teams. We say, "Why can't all the kids play? Why does the coach put only the talented kids into the game, while the other kids sit on the bench?" And then we complain that the coach pushes the kids too hard to win. They have to be right all the time, they aren't supposed to make errors. The horror of that on the athletic field comes home to us and yet we act the same way in our homes. We push for excellence in our children in regard to their marks, their homework, their rooms, their table manners, their friends, their opinions, or whatever gets us upset. We are pretty sure coaches are fulfilling their own dreams and ambitions through those kids, but what are we doing? The same thing at home—trying to fulfill our dreams and ambitions.

It's far more important that the child know what's good about him than what's bad about him. They don't know their strong points and how good they truly are. The best way we can help them recognize their strengths is by giving our approval. It isn't enough to be aware of how frequently or scathingly we criticize and of our resolve to change. We have to know with our heads and believe deep in our hearts that children grow with praise. Praise is the sunlight and moisture that brings our children to full bloom. Even if we feel that our children know that we think they're good, we should praise them again and again. They never hear enough. We're so hesitant. Are we afraid our children will become proud? That is the least of our worries.

Tony and Mary told me how their eighth anniversary signaled a change in their lives. Mary had looked forward all day to Tony's coming home and their going to the restaurant where they had first met, but while they were dressing he'd yelled at the children and all the vibrancy had gone out of her. Tony was always putting them down. Over and over he took the joy out of their lives by criticizing them—and her. He could always find their weak points and let them know about them.

Her eyes filled with tears and she shook her head. She didn't want to cry. He'd start yelling about her being too sensitive, that he wanted to get going and how she was such a slowpoke. Boy, he was mean. Suddenly, the thought struck her that it wasn't a one-way street. She was also pretty good at doling out sharp little comments.

Mary had hurriedly put on her makeup and slipped into her dress. Later that evening over dessert she said, "Tony, why don't we give each other a special anniversary present this year, one that could make us happy for a long time? You know how we pick at the kids and each other? Let's give that up for this year. We're always pointing out what's wrong and letting everybody know when we're displeased. Why not spend this year pointing out what's good with each other and letting everybody know when we're pleased?"

Tony took her up on it, and although neither was perfect, a year later back at their restaurant again—but this time with the whole family—Tony toasted his wife. "To Mary, who always has a lot of good ideas, but last year had the best one ever. We knocked off being on each other's back and the kids' backs and we started finding out one another's good points. Kids, you're great. We're so proud of you! This has been the happiest year of my life!"

Pop, who ran the restaurant, brought out a decorated cake with candles, as he always did on people's birthdays. Tony told him no one had a birthday. Pop answered, "I know, I know, but you're all so happy—I say it's everybody's birthday!"

The greatest endowment any person can receive is praise. If we find nothing to praise in our children, we have that magnifying glass of criticism out again; we're not looking at the diamond, we're looking for flaws. The problem is not in our children, the problem is in us—the way we are looking at them. Every one of our children, whether we think so or not, is always praiseworthy.

What would help you praise your children more and criticize them less?

Your answer:

First, we need to honestly and sincerely come to grips with the importance of praise. It is more helpful, longer lasting and more effective than anything else we can do for our children.

Second, we need to recognize that we're far more accustomed to criticizing than praising. Whether we criticize explicitly and harshly or subtly and gently, criticism looms larger in our relationship with our children than praise.

Third, we must follow the advice, *"When you open your mouth to criticize, close it."*

Fourth, we must reverse the pattern of criticizing by being conscious of the children's good points and show our appreciation of them with words and actions.

Are we afraid that in order to praise our children we'll have to make up things? That we'll be phony? There is no occasion for fear on that account. If we pay attention to the good things about the children, the praise will be real!

Our problem is that we're like the fellow on the tennis court who didn't return the ball and looked at his racket as though the strings were missing. But the strings were there, he just hadn't made contact. The same thing is true as far as finding things to praise in our children. They're there, we just haven't made contact.

To make contact we can take time to think of nice things about our children. What do we like most about them? What are their best qualities? We can build them up in our minds and think of ways to express the positive view to them. As we care, they will come to know that these good things about them are important and recognized.

The best way to praise them is to be specific. If we speak in general saying, "You're a nice boy," or, "You're a good girl," it doesn't accomplish much; we are not convincing. By being specific about when the child was patient or thoughtful, sensitive, understanding or attentive, then he knows we did notice, and he is pleased. Children who are so praised begin to have confidence that those good qualities are really theirs!

Our kids are terrific and we tell them

Discipline is helping our children grow into making decisions for themselves.

4

DISCIPLINE

**Why do you
discipline
your children?**

Your answer:

We discipline our children for all kinds of reasons—so they won't hurt themselves, so they won't make the mistakes we did, they disobeyed, they have to learn to behave better, they have to learn to take orders, it's our duty, they embarrass us when they misbehave, the neighbors will think poorly of us if we let the children run wild, there's got to be order in the house.

We could add many more. Most of them aim for immediate peace and harmony, meaning the absence of friction or "war." But none of them are the right reasons for making rules and following through. All of these are focused on conduct and control, orders and rewards (in small letters) and punishment (in capital letters). Discipline is actually reduced to enforced activity—with a lot of punishment. Discipline is much more than that. It should help the child grow into making proper decisions for himself. We want him to become a responsible person, one who is able to respond to people and to circumstances in proper ways.

The discipline that we exert on our children comes from the values we have in life. Through our discipline we are communicating our values and at the same time calling to our children to respond to us and our love. It is concerned with how our children understand us and care about understanding us, how they treasure what we treasure. Discipline is concerned with what the child thinks of himself and how he regards his relationship with us. That is something far deeper than whether or not the child did or didn't do a particular chore at a given moment.

A rule should be put in for the sake of building up that relationship. Of course family relationships can't be created by rules, but rules can support the relationship that a family is building. They can help us become more of a family! For example, we might put in the rule, "Everyone has to be home for supper at 6:00." The rule can be put in because we have to have dinner sometime and we've decided to eat at 6:00 and get it over with. Or, it can be put in because we really want to enjoy one another and, naturally, we want everybody present. If we truly want it for the sake of family unity, then we will think of family unity and make the meal interesting and attractive, and we'll care about each member of the family. If we don't spend any time with one another at the meal, if we just eat fast and get out, or let one member monopolize the conversation, or let it be a time for griping or arguing or picking at one another, we're not serious about building up the relationship of the family. Then a father and mother and their children can be several persons who are living in the same house and not be a "family." One of the advantages of discipline is that it gets us beyond that; we get to be people involved, caring about one another.

It is a great challenge to think of discipline as those things that will help build harmony and develop our well-being and the growth and enjoyment of our family life together! Then the children are richly endowed for all their lives.

How is discipline handled in your home?   *Your answer:*

(Here's a check list for you.)

What do you expect discipline to accomplish?

Does your discipline vary according to the age and capability of each child?

Do you have an overview of discipline?

Do you play favorites with the children?

Are you looking for the children to be successful (obedient), or are you trying to "catch" them?

Are you always trying to correct what's wrong, or are you affirming what's right and strengthening the child in that, increasing his sphere of right-doing?

Do other people, specifically grandparents, influence your discipline?

Do you look for other people such as the teacher at school to provide the discipline you lack?

Does the success or failure of other children in the fmaily influence the way you're disciplining a child now? (Perhaps an older child caused a lot of problems, so we crack down on the younger children, or maybe an older child is very good, so we set him up as a paragon. We expect all the other children to live up to him.)

Are you independent in your discipline, or have you imposed it upon the children in order to have the approval of relatives or neighbors?

Are you locked into following books or authorities on discipline?

Do you give the children a chance to be heard, or is your discipline automatic and authoritarian?

Are you willing to risk being fooled occasionally in order to give the children room to breathe?

Do you use the child's past failures to determine his present discipline?

Does your child frequently accuse you of not trusting him? (This can't be answered by saying, "Of course I trust you." Either we don't trust the child or he is not experiencing our trust. Either shows that an atmosphere of distrust has been created between ourselves and the child. Of course, we can't let the child do anything he wants to do, but we must begin again to build our relationship positively.)

What motivation are you offering the children to "obey the rules"? Is it fear? The fear of physical violence or the deprivation of a privilege? Or the fear that you will withdraw your approval? Is it guilt? If he doesn't do such and such, he ought to be ashamed? Or is the motive your pleasure? The desire to please you and be appreciated?

Do your emotions dictate your discipline?

Do you let the child's reaction determine your stick-to-it-iveness? (When the child gets too upset, we lessen the punishment or back off entirely.)

Do you try to help the child understand the reasons behind your discipline so that he knows that more than external comformity is important?

Are you doing anything specific to make sure the children are growing in their thinking and feeling about your values?

How much time do you give to discipline? Do you anticipate the problems your children are going to face, the values you are trying to inculcate or the situations that the child is likely to face within the next couple of months? Or do you wait until circumstances or events come up—and then are overwhelmed by them?

Are your children a part of the whole process of rule-making and follow through or do you tell them the net results of your discussions when the event occurs? In other words, does he see the merit of positive behavior before he gets into trouble?

We can discover how we are doing by observing how our oldest child deals with the younger children when he watches over them. He reveals how he experienced us! They're less subtle than we are and usually more rigid and unyielding, but they pretty much want their brothers and sisters to do what we've wanted them to do. His

We hope Wendy sees that a lot of caring goes into mediating a quarrel.

actions will open our eyes, but he is at a decided disadvantage. He will be "bossy," only wanting obedience. Parents' true authority depends on the children's responsiveness; they want a caring relationship to develop between themselves and their children.

Do you follow through? *Your answer:*

We often shout out loud and clear what a rule is or what we expect of the children and then don't do anything about it. It's not because we don't want to follow through, but we're distracted or we're too busy or we just aren't up to it. Or maybe we happen to be in a good mood and what we wanted done yesterday and "forever" isn't all that important today. Of course the issue itself may not make much difference, but the whole process of disciplining demands attention to detail! Unfortunately we find it easier to be sprinters than long-distance runners.

A rule which is put down and then not insisted upon is training in the negative. To tell children that we expect a very definite action done or not done and then not be bothered if that rule is violated is unfair. What are they to think? If our rules are chosen for the well-being of the child and the advancement of family life, then we better be involved and follow through.

When there is a problem with follow-through on the part of either of us or both, it may be that we don't really believe in the rule we've made. In that case, follow-through is not the problem, it's a symptom. The problem may be one of wanting the child's affection and approval all the time. We don't enforce the rule because that makes Johnny unhappy and he doesn't "like" us. That is a sad state of affairs!

So, we shouldn't make a rule unless we mean it. We're in trouble if we shoot from the lip and establish a rule when actually all we want is something done at the moment. That's not a rule; that is a specific request.

A rule is something that should be done over an extended period of time on a consistent basis. Our rules should not come out of single needs, because we won't be able to follow through and shouldn't. For instance, one morning I have to get out of the house to a meeting and I want everything in order beforehand. I get so upset that I overstate the case and put in a rule, "Beds have to be made by 7:30 every morning!"

So, it becomes a big thing in the family that beds have to be made by 7:30. But most other days it doesn't matter. Follow-through is difficult and unadvisable under those circumstances. It's better to rethink the rule.

When it is necessary to impose a punishment, that shouldn't mean that the child is rejected. The punishment has to be applied and has to be done with firmness, but life has to go on. The child shouldn't be put in a position of being embarrassed or put out in left field until the punishment has been finished. More so at this time than any other, it's important to praise him for the good things and to celebrate his fine qualities in other areas of the relationship within the family. Otherwise, we are inconsistent. He has messed up in only one area, so we need to keep the punishment there, recognizing and reaffirming the child's goodnesses. To be consistent we apply the punishment where it's deserved and we give the rewards and joy where it's deserved.

Do you support each other?

Your answer:

Most of us do our best to be of one mind in front of the children, but we let our differences show when we are apart. We need to support each other when we are not in each other's presence. A wife who goes along with a rule when her husband is home and doesn't during the day when he's at work is doing more than cheating a little. By letting the children be outside the rule so long as her husband doesn't find out about it, is teaching a value of expediency, that disobeying is only bad if one gets caught!

There are less obvious ways of not supporting each other that may trip us up. We may back up exactly what our spouse has said, whether he's around or not, but then do some things to compensate the children for what we think is an unreasonable or too harsh rule. And it could happen the opposite way. We think a rule is too lenient, so in order to discipline the children we put in some other rules to make up for its lack.

We will also undercut what the other person has said if we don't get involved with the disciplining of the children. If we just wash our hands of the whole thing, we're not being supportive. The other person needs to know that he's really being backed. We have to be actively involved, not just in saying to the kids, "Do what your mother (or father) tells you to do," but in talking it over together, both knowing what's involved, helping each other and backing each other 100%. We diminish our relationship with the children when we don't stand united. If we only pretend to be united, the nonverbal communication and body language tell the child that we disagree. The oneness we strive for runs deep. We will blend with each other in all ways so that we instinctively react harmoniously in our relationships with the children. It's not good enough to decide on the particular things we'll insist on, what privileges we'll give, and what type of punishments we'll mete out to the children. We have to be in harmony about the values we're trying to communicate. If we're looking ahead and planning together, we can have a genuine blending—a common position that we can apply to the children with peace and harmony.

This is going to take time, a lot of conversation, a lot of being open to each other in the peace of "ahead of time." Feelings will be talked about, and goals and values and authority and rules and

Everything happens at once when you are gone but — the lawn's raked and everybody got to bed at a reasonable time.

Hurry home!

122

what to do about infractions. There's no way this can be accomplished by one sit-down, nor can it be accomplished by just facing issues as they come up.

As we meld together, our subconscious feelings can surface. Maybe we've undercut each other in the past because we don't quite trust our spouse. It isn't that we think the other person is bad, we just think he is mistaken or hasn't our values or that we are superior in some way. Frequently the mother thinks that because she's around the youngsters so much she knows them much better than the father. But it's also true that a father feels the mother is with them so much that she's not very good at disciplining so he has to take over.

"Wait until your father comes home," is not supporting the father in his role in discipline. What it is doing is making him the heavy. Equally bad, it delays the punishment, and delayed punishment is not good. So, when one of us has to act on his own, we need to tell the other what we've asked of the children. It's unfair for one parent to be in the position of reacting to a situation, not knowing what has gone before. When we don't inform each other, a child is encouraged to manipulate us, and we get into a conflict situation or at best a dutiful support one.

Here is something else that is very important. We should be praising our spouse in front of the children often—when he's present and when he isn't. We can describe the goodness of the other person, his values and why he's doing the things he is. Then we'll come across in total harmony. If all we do to support our spouse is to agree with him in front of the children, our support will be incomplete, uneven and, questionable. For example, a little girl having been spanked by her mother comes to her father. Of course she's playing for sympathy—and there's nothing wrong with the father giving her sympathy and understanding—but in the course of it, he should explain the values they are trying to teach the child and why the mother was so upset. In order to do that, the husband and wife will have had to talk a lot! In this case, he will not even have to get specific word from his wife about what happened, he will already know! He can explain to the child what went on because he knows them both well. In doing so, he is also reinforcing how much Mommy loves the child even though she has just been spanked. He needs to resist the implication that he loves that little girl more than Mommy does even at this specific time by talking about how much Mommy cares for her.

Truly supporting each other comes from a genuine blending of hearts and a real empathizing with our beloved. And both of us will be taking responsibility for the development of our children.

What part does authority play in your discipline?

Your answer:

A parent, in the nature of his being a parent, has power to require and receive submission. The two-year-old who runs across the street without looking needs a loud commanding voice and a broad hand on his bottom. We are to expect obedience from our children, but we may or may not get it. If we give orders and force our children to fulfill them, we are no more than dictators. If our children know that we love them and find us to be trustworthy and competent, fair and strong of character, they will respect us and acknowledge us as the persons in the family who carry the authority. They will be more inclined to obey willingly.

That type of authority is not "control" or "power" with a heavy hand which doesn't allow for personal relationships. Rather it is a mutual respect, love and responsiveness between us and our children because of our concern for them and our awareness of one another's goodness.

True authority has more to do with reverence and love than with obedience. If we reduce children to obeying us because they have to, there is something wrong with our relationship. Actually, strict obedience is not an ideal for which to strive. It should never be an issue. The ideal is to have the youngsters respond to us because they want to please us and want to grow closer to us. It may be easier for us to give orders, "Do it because I say so," and insist on our way, but that approach is self-defeating. When they are old enough to say no, they will. We can see this all around us.

As the children go into adulthood, the relationship between them and their parents becomes more and more minimal. That's bad. When the child gets out of the inferior position of being forced— by word and action—to be obedient, then the parent no longer has "authority."

We have a different kind of problem when we exercise authority for our sake and not for the sake of the child. We express it this way. "Look, as long as you live in this house, this is the way you act." The implication is that the child can do anything he wants when he lives outside the house because then it won't bother us. We're saying that we really don't care about his good. But if something is wrong, it is wrong whether it's done in Chicago or in San Francisco, whether it's done in our house or in an apartment far away.

There is another negative side to using our authority to threaten punishment or withhold a privilege as the motivation for obedience. We have to be present. On the other hand, if the motivation for obedience is love for us, then they'll do it whether we're present or not.

Also, if our authority is dependent upon our always being right, then we have to be infallible. No one is that, even though we often give the children the impression that we are!

If we have equated authority with getting our way— "Everybody in this house has to conform to what I think and want done"—we're putting our convictions and comfort first. That's tyranny, not parenthood. We are not facing into our children and recognizing that there is supposed to be a "family" relationship.

We should encourage our children to respond to us because we are "us"—because of who we are to them, personally. True authority is personal. When the child does something not because he has to or because it's right, but because of what it means to us, beautiful things happen. Strangely that's difficult to accept. We would rather have the children do something because it's right. That sounds admirable, and of course we intend that what we want done *is* right, but we do things for the sake of the person we trust, respect and love. If we can teach our children that concept of authority, the rebellious mentality so present in our society will cease.

Knowledge is a part of exercising authority. If we shield ourselves from the input necessary to make adequate decisions, then

They want to please us. That makes our days super.

implicitly we surrender our authority. For example, I may be boss in my business but if I don't know what's going on then the decisions will have to be made by someone who is knowledgeable. The same thing is true in the home. If I don't know what the kids are doing, what's going on in school or in the neighborhood then I'm hardly in a position to have an opinion—much less to be able to engage in the decision-making process.

Authority fundamentally is an expression of a personal relationship. It consists of persons having influence with other persons. Those who influence us are ones we listen to carefully and whose opinions we reverence. They aren't making up our minds for us, making our decisions or imposing their will upon us. Our response to them can be considered a gift to them.

It can be that we maintain the façade of authority and never achieve influence over our children. We win our points but we lose our influence; influence is the key element in the relationship.

Once authority is introduced into a discussion between two people, the personal relationship takes a back seat and superior-inferior comes to the forefront. The personal relationship is abandoned. We become closed off to each other. It is usually because we lack security that we protect ourselves with a mantle of authority and demand obedience and external conformity.

When we put our authority on the line and say, "This is my house; while you're in this house you will do what I say," we miss the whole point. This is a home and our children belong here just as much as we do. The reason we have the responsibility for insisting upon discipline is not because we pay the bills, it's because we have the experience, the background, the education, the training and the thoughtfulness to be able to point out things that the children have not yet experienced.

What part does consistency play?

Your answer:

The most important single aspect of discipline is consistency. Our children need guidelines that are constant. If they are always shifting, the children will have no base—they will feel insecure and their moral principles will be chaotic. They will not be developing discipline in their own lives. For us to have one set of rules one day and another set of rules the next day doesn't make sense. Nor does it if on one occasion we react strongly to a violation of a certain rule and on another we ignore it—or just give a tiny slap on the wrist. That's training the child that there are no real norms in this world, that what they do only depends on external circumstances. This leads to a discipline that's wishy-washy, subjective. We take away the strong, objective quality of the discipline.

Take a simple thing like bedtime. In many homes it's a big hassle. We ought to look at what the child is doing—he's not going to bed—and look at ourselves to find out how this pattern developed. We'll almost certainly discover we've been inconsistent in explaining to the children that we have serious feelings about bedtime. We may rant and rave on Monday night that they must be in bed by 8:30, but the next night when we're absorbed in a TV drama, we pretend not to notice that the children are still up. Maybe the next night we're on the phone, so we don't bother with the children being out of bed. But on the fourth night we're not occupied, so we hit the ceiling again. We say, "Now we really mean this," but the children don't believe us because we didn't mean it on Tuesday and Wednesday.

There's another side of bedtime where consistency is needed. One of us feels like playing with the kids at bedtime and the other has to be the heavy by insisting that they go to bed. The children don't know what is expected of them or to whom to respond. And sometimes our reaction to one child may be different than that toward another. We may be strict with the six-year-old and say he must go to bed because he needs his sleep. But we let the four-year-old stay up because she's so cute. The six-year-old is smart enough to wonder why he needs his sleep and the younger one doesn't.

As the children grow older, time becomes more and more important to us. One of the ways to avoid complications is to have rules based on action lines. If 10 p.m. is set down as the absolute time when a child must be home, whatever the action, there can be problems. Far better that a reasonable amount of time be allowed after the particular event for the son or daughter to stop and have ice cream. One event may be over at 9:30, another at 12:00! Decide what the reasonable time is for the child to come home from school without having to run home and get into the house at the earliest possible opportunity. If supper is at 6:00, we can emphasize that the child should be home so that we can all be together. The emphasis is on the family gathering rather than on the clock. A child could be home at 6:00 and be a bear with the family. The times are different; the principle involved is the same. All too often we make some kind of a magic out of a certain time. We feel that if the child is in by 12:00 nothing is going to happen. That's just not true.

How much better to educate the children so that whether they are outside the home or inside, they conduct themselves according to certain principles! We may take away any choice from a child to make sure he can't do anything wrong, but sooner or later—on whatever level it is—he is capable of doing it by himself, whether it's robbing the cookie jar at six or going to bed with a girl at 16.

A couple can be consistent and not be rigid. The letter of the law doesn't have to be applied irrevocably on every single occasion exactly the same way. Within a given framework, there can be an openness to the spirit of the discipline and a flexibility to respond to the needs of the individual child. This will not weaken the consistency of the discipline. It will recognize that discipline is not a harsh legalism.

It is especially important when our child has a particular need. When we listen and respond to him rather than just applying a rule because it's a rule, we're exercising judgment and considering the highest value of all—his personhood. We'll all make mistakes, but each member of the family has different needs at different times. As much as we need to be consistent with rules, it is more important to be consistent in our love toward the child and respond to him. For example, a family rule may be, "Homework is to be out of the way before supper." That's not so bad. It gives a child time to unwind before going to bed and he's not so tense and heavy when he's to go to sleep. But suppose on a given day a child comes home and he's had a bad day. Everything has gone wrong. He needs to unwind right then and be fussed over a little and maybe needs the privilege of watching TV or just playing with his friends. He'll do better if this time homework can wait until after supper. The next day if all goes all right at school, we enforce the rule. There will be no problems if we and our spouse are one in the way we look at discipline.

To be consistent, parents need to be one in mind, one in heart, and one in affection. It's important that a mother and father get away from being two individuals who happen to get along pretty well as far as disciplining the children is concerned and develop "couple" consistency. That's better than two approaches to discipline which are compatible.

How has your past influenced your discipline?

Your answer:

The way that we deal with our children will be shaped more or less by the memories of the way our parents dealt with us. We may be just as strict or as lenient as they were, or we may act in the opposite way. We may so over-react to what we consider a very strict upbringing that we provide no discipline at all—we just sort of let our children go! If we feel we were held down and not allowed to do a lot of fun things, we can have the impression that loving our children is to give them everything they want. If we had a parent we didn't respect because we saw him as weak, we may resolve to be different and become harsh and demanding.

Maybe we are carrying a history as an older child or as the youngest or middle child that prejudices us in our relationship with our children. Maybe our past was lonely and the bitter experiences are so strong that we want to make sure our children don't go through the same thing. Maybe we are idealizing our home life in the past in such a way that we're trying to create a "somewhere over the rainbow" scene. We have an exaggerated view of the goodness of our mother and father and are trying slavishly to imitate what we think they did. We might, even now, allow our parents to influence the disciplining of our children so that we aren't developing our own values or making our own decisions.

Probably the most serious mistake we make in our relationship with our children is to try to treat them as we think we wanted to be treated. It's an appealing idea, but there are two serious drawbacks. First of all, we may think we have an accurate recollection of our childhood, but we don't. Our memory is made up of many individual incidents that have blended into a pattern. (By the same token, in order to avoid a single individual incident, we may be creating a whole opposite pattern.) Second, we imply that our children are exactly like us. We assume that because we wanted to be treated a certain way, our child will want the same. That is not necessarily true. Our discipline has to be custom-made for our children. It has to respond to the children as they are, not as we think we were.

Although we learn from our past experience in childhood, we have to be careful to recognize that our children are in many ways different from us and from each other, and that we are not the same people as our parents.

(We have a terrific opportunity to show our children how we

are dealing with our own parents now. We can tell a lot about our past and explain what we appreciated then and appreciate now. By our having an environment and atmosphere with our parents that is good, warm and loving, our children will benefit more than we can possibly imagine.)

What kinds of rules don't work for you?

Your answer:

Rules or goals that the children can't attain are usually unreasonable ones. If we say, "You should get A's," we're assuming that the child is bright enough and has no problems. However, if he just isn't up to A work or his talents don't quite fit the teacher's idea of an A student, it's unreasonable to expect A's. In the busyness of our lives we make many demands on our children without much thought—ride a bike, play ball, socialize. Of course we hope they can enjoy those things—we especially want our children to be friends with everybody in the neighborhood—but there are some children who can do them at a certain age and others who can't. We're setting a rule that cannot be successful.

We also set up objectives that can't be met when we tell an eight-year-old to make sure his little brother or sister does something. We may say, "Make sure you take your little brother along when you go out to play with your friends." Well, maybe the friends just won't accept the little brother, so Tommy has to forget about playing with his friends or he disobeys you. It's too difficult a dilemma for the child.

Neither can we enforce, "Don't wet the bed tonight," "Don't bite your nails." "Don't spill things," "Don't touch." Youngsters' motor coordination and eye sight isn't fully developed, and what are they supposed to do with their hands? It'd be wise to give them some things they can touch in exchange for what we tell them not to touch. "Stay clean" is another beautiful one, and, "Be good," whatever that means.

When an older child digs in his heels and refuses to obey a rule, even when the rule is reasonable and important, and we hold to it, it creates an environment of constant friction and hostility and private withdrawal that is terrible. In the face of that we might give up and let the child do anything he wants. Both reactions are wrong. Instead of doing either one and getting emotionally upset, we need to introduce a different campaign to accomplish what is necessary. We need to lay out long-term goals and long-term accomplishments. That will relieve the tension and give a fresh start.

Rules of overstatement don't work very well. They are caused by something like this: a child uses a toy improperly—by hitting another kid over the head with it or using it for a hammer—and you say, "Okay, you can't play with that any more." First of all, that doesn't solve the problem. The child has to learn what is the appropriate activity for that toy, and he'll never learn what it is if the toy is taken away. Second, what does "any more" mean? Forever? A week or two? Rules need to be specific and within the understanding of the child. Because open-ended rules are difficult for a child to understand (and we don't always know what we mean) they are hard to follow through on. What tends to happen is that we don't let the child play with the toy for a while—a few hours, a few days. After we cool down we say, "Well, he's learned his lesson," but the lesson the child has learned is that if he waits long enough he'll get the toy back. If "patience in the face of adversity" is the value we want to teach, then we've made a beginning. It takes awhile to learn what our follow-through capabilities are and we'll make mistakes, but it's worth sticking with.

The rules that work, we need to keep. The ones that don't, we need to rethink—throw out if necessary—so that we can try again.

What kinds of punishment don't work?

Your answer:

Punishing children with the silent treatment seems like a good idea, but it is cruel. It creates a whole environment of heaviness, a constant atmosphere that is oppressive. We would never hit our youngsters for an extended period of time. Any punishment that's called for should be applied quickly, and the relationship restored as soon as possible. Silence doesn't allow for that.

Another poor form of punishment is to make the other person conscious of how badly he makes us feel or how much he has hurt us. If we make our child feel guilty by telling him how unappreciative he is, how he's always thinking of himself and being unkind, we drive home to him that he's a bad person, even evil. That's wrong.

Long-term punishments are cruelty.

Punishing with physical force is dangerous. What might appear as a light blow can be a heavy one to a little child. (Actually,

Forgive us for knocking out the dining room lights with the spray hose.

physical force—swift and strong, but careful—is best used as an attention-getter and a reminder! It isn't sufficient in itself. We need to sit down and talk with the child and then be reconciled with him. The more the physical punishment, the more the physical affection that has to follow it. Then the child recognizes that it is the wrong activity in which he has been engaged that is being rejected, not he.)

The postponed punishment is cruelty. Young children don't comprehend anything beyond a couple of minutes from now. Even older children have trouble conceiving of time. Punishment should be immediate, quick and over with.

What values do you want to teach your children?

Your answer:

We all want to teach our children to value truth, beauty, fairness, honor, fidelity, strength of character, loyalty, integrity, independence—the beautiful values. We discipline our children to tell the truth, to match their clothes, to share their toys, to cut the cake in equal pieces, to keep their promises, to not throw stones at anyone, to salute the flag, to stand up for what is right and to think on their own. We also want them to care about getting a respectable job and having a good life. These are fine qualities, but they can be very lonely ones, for they are often limited to the personal, individual aspects of life. A person could have them to the hilt and go to his grave a respected lonely warrior who spent his life being true to himself. That is tragic. We can do better. We can raise our children to stress the side of values that prepares them to face the world—not so much as individuals—but as "family."

We can teach them dependence. In our society we look on dependence as weakness, as a sign of inadequacy, when the truth is, if we can't be dependent on someone else's love, then we can never have a full relationship. What about trust? How much of a value do we consider trust to be? The tragic reality in our alienated society is that we don't have neighborhoods any more and our children have to be trained to protect themselves from aberrant elements. We are actually teaching them to be distrustful. Maybe we have become too concerned about protecting our children. They keep to themselves even in the most intimate and open circumstances!

How highly do we value communication (which results in beautiful personal relationships) versus accomplishment? We look on people who get along well with others and have mediocre careers as unsuccessful. We talk about life passing them by. However, the real sadness should be reserved for those with great careers and mediocre relationships!

What values are you actually teaching your children?

Your answer:

One of the first values we establish in the disciplining of our children is self-preservation. It's in terms of, "Don't touch the stove," "Don't cross the street," "Don't put your finger in the electric light socket." It's a whole series of "don'ts." But with them the child begins the process of learning that there are dangers to his life and he has to take measures to preserve himself, that he has to deny himself things that are attractive for the higher value which is his life.

Then there is the value of fairness. When he begins to play with other children, we discipline him to share. Each child gets a fair amount of whatever is being done. If it's having cookies, each gets the same number; if it's a toy, each has his time to play with it.

We may want to teach our children all kinds of fine values and talk a lot about spiritual values and the merits of personal relationships, but our actions belie our words. We seem more concerned that our children make a living than enjoy living. Do we really want them to be breadwinners rather than family people? The family is the core of society. Yet we teach that other values are primary and imply that the family can be taken for granted. Home life should not take second place to the other elements in life—a job, a cause or anything. And yet, it is only when there are no demands upon us that we want our youngsters' companionship or their affection and are interested in the subjects they want to talk about. But then the circumstances change and we react differently. If we're not up to their noise and we demand peace and quiet, the overriding value we communicate is that life is about gaining personal comfort and convenience. Concern for one's own well-being is more important than the children.

When we're uptight about the amount of money we make or our advancement with a company or the type of home we can afford, we transmit an overriding ambition to our children to get ahead in life. This is often translated into an intense drive for education. There are two factors here. First, education becomes a tool for material or professional advancement instead of a way to develop a capacity for self-realization and an opportunity to open various possibilities for personal fulfillment. Second, it equates human development and happiness in life with climbing up the corporate ladder, a very shaky perch from which to face life.

So, through our instructions we may be teaching materialism, indifference to others, selfishness, self-centeredness, without our being aware of it. We can't be too condemnatory of ourselves on this because we are a mixture of values, and it may very well be that we actually have more material values than we realize or would like to admit. But there can also be some very real personal or spiritual values down deep. If we value listening, whether we are aware of it in so many words or not, our discipline will give these experiences to our children and they will value listening. That value will last and enrich them through depression and prosperity, through war and peace, through sickness and health, until old age. Sensitivity, gentleness, understanding, are values that never wear out. We can never be pensioned off for those qualities. We can never be fired for those capabilities. We can

Our loving each other is the best gift we can give to our children.

never be rejected for them. Everybody treasures those along with honor, integrity, faithfulness, love of God. No human being with those values engrained in them could fail. Their external circumstances might be poor, but there'd be so much fullness within them they could overcome anything!

When I was growing up it was very clear to me that my mother was the religious one in the family. I knew my father was a good man, and he went to church faithfully, but my mother did many more spiritual things and talked a lot more about it. When I entered the seminary I gradually came to realize that faith was every bit as important to my father as it was to my mother. More importantly, I recognized that their whole relationship with each other revolved around their faith. It was one of the things they found most attractive in each other. It was faith that bound them together and made me who I am.

What about the values of a sympathetic heart and an understanding ear, or the capacity to fully reveal ourselves to people we're close to? How high are these values in our hierarchy of values? They have far more to do with the success of a love relationship than any other qualities we can think of.

And there's nothing more important in this world than love.

When we equip our children to love and accept love, we are giving them the most important of all values and they'll know what being a couple and being parents is all about. That is the ultimate value we have to share with our children, the importance of a love relationship in life. We can't just tell them that, we have to live it. Values are not memorized, they are experienced. Love—loving and being loved—is treasured because it is the deepest of all human values. It is irresistible.

Are you a friend to your children?   *Your answer:*

We all want to be on a friendly basis with our children. And we are when we have a close, warm, affectionate relationship with them. But should we relate to our youngsters in the same way as buddy to buddy or girlfriend to girlfriend? "Friends" approve of each other. "Friends" basically agree with each other and support each other's positions. If they don't, we hear, "He (or she) is not my friend!" Parents and their children have a different relationship. They have ties that hold them above and beyond that of approval. One of the beautiful things about family life is that the ties are so strong and the experience of one another so deep that other bonds are unnecessary. At the same time, parents don't have to insist upon respect because of their age or position, for the children respect them and the parents respect their children because of a mutual responsiveness that is based on deep communication and a deep commitment to one another.

What is the best attitude to have in disciplining your children?   *Your answer:*

We are not a prefect of discipline. We haven't received job assignments to be fulfilled through our youngsters. We've not been made wardens. We're persons who love our boys and girls. Our tenderness for them is the most evident aspect of our whole relationship with them. More than anything else we're concerned with their well-being and, above all, their happiness. Too often in discipline, we come across to the children as reducing their happiness. They may recognize that we sincerely believe the discipline is for their good, and they may even admit that it is for their good, but it comes across as joyless. To change that, we can honestly be concerned about their joy. It isn't just that we're concerned that our children not be hurt. We have to positively look for their happiness and their fullness of life. If our children honestly and sincerely believe that we want them to enjoy everything they possibly can in life, then they'll be much more willing to listen to us. Furthermore, our choice of restrictions and expectations is going to be more human and realistic. Basic to all of them will be our oneness.

The attitude of oneness in a family touches everything in the home. While some things are used primarily by a particular member, most things are used by the whole family. We all appreciate the living room, we all eat at the table, we all enjoy the tub, the TV and the yard. Those are "community" property. However, a stereo, new carpeting or a white chair may be declared off limits. Denying certain possessions to a youngster, teaches him that the possession comes before him. It also establishes that it is the parents' private property, it's not a family thing. We have these possessions and you can't touch them. (But any possessions of yours, of course, I can touch!) When we divide off areas of mine and yours and theirs, we're not "family" any more. Better to maintain the attitude of "community" and teach responsibility. "The stereo belongs to all of us, we all can enjoy and appreciate it. Dad and Mom will operate it, and Billy can, too, when he has learned how."

If we can deal with our children with ease and humor and gentleness, everything will go better. And optimism is contagious! By the same token, if we're convinced that our youngsters are going to fail—that they're going to let us down—we're likely to have a self-fulfilling prophecy and they will! Expecting their cooperation and success and assuming it's there, great things can

It's time for bed — but the world won't fall apart if we settle problems first.

happen. If they don't have a cooperative spirit we need to develop that first. We don't want to be apart from our child, with a wall between us. We're not role-playing. We're loving our children. The highest motivation for our responding to other people is to have a desire to please them, to want to be part of the other person's life. We will do things that are important to them. So, in order to get that across to our children, we have to provide them with the opportunity to desire to please us. That will come only if they can see that we're on their side. Above all, we have to be on their side!

It's easy for children to believe that parents are against them or at least against their freedom or that they just don't understand what are the important things in life to children. After all, they see us dealing with life seriously, dutifully, and always trying to get them to fulfill their duties. If Jesus comes to us and tells us that He came to bring us life and to bring us more abundant life, isn't that what we should be giving to our children? We are to show them how they can get more out of life! How to enjoy it!

Would you say your children are well-disciplined?

Your answer:

Most parents would answer that question, and they really wouldn't be answering it! If they said yes, they might mean that their children are well-behaved. But good behavior can come about because of all sorts of external pressures and factors plus an internal climate of passivity or an inclination toward compliance. A well-disciplined child has developed self-discipline. He has the strength that allows him, according to his age and growth, to determine how he's going to exercise the values in his life. So, in a sense, someone could be poorly-behaved and well-disciplined, and somebody else could be very well-behaved and have no discipline at all.

Some children play the "letter of the law" game with their parents and say, "But you told me that I must do this," and the parents' response is "Yes, but anybody with commonsense could see that it doesn't apply in these circumstances." Both are giving the facts, but the reason the child is at a disadvantage is because he has not had the opportunity to develop self-discipline. He has not interiorized values as far as this particular situation is concerned. He is behavior-oriented, or he has run up against a situation which calls for more discernment than he is capable of.

What are some steps toward good discipline that you can take now?

Your answer:

1. *We need to figure out what values—what goals—we want to set up for our children both for now and the future.*
2. *We need to evaluate our motivation.* Why do we want our children to have these particular values and goals?
3. *We need to fit the rules to each child's ability and understanding.* His capability to perform will increase—it's a process. It takes time to assimilate a value, so we can't just lay down a rule, give our explanation and walk away from it. It has to be explained over and over again in different ways so that the child gradually assimilates our reasoning.
4. *We need to give more consideration to follow through.* If we have any doubts of our attainment in this area, we should adjust the rules.
5. *We need to realize that there will be some failure on the part of the children.* None of us ever take on new things and accomplish them right away, whether it's riding a bicycle or reading or even walking. And each child is different, so the execution of our expectation will be expressed differently by each one. Sometimes we think a child is not living up to his potential. His potential for what? Two children can have the same IQ and have totally different potentials. It's not a question of brightness or intellectual power. A person is much more than his intellect. There are whole complexes of talents, capabilities and capacities that are involved.
6. *We need to associate with other parents of like values.* As we talk over our purposes, our problems, our experiences, with them, they will encourage, inspire and open new horizons to us. And we will do the same for them!
7. *We need to open our hearts, do away with our fears and accept the children's doing things for us.* The highest motivation that any child can have in responding to a request that we make is to be doing it for us! It isn't necessary that they know all about it's being the right thing to do. Of course we feel that the thing is

objectively right, and we want them to grow in understanding of a moral obligation, but doing it only on that basis means that we're not personally involved. We might say, "Well, what will they do when we're not here any more? Then will they have any motivation to do the right thing?" But we are never gone from our children. We may be dead many years, but we're still very present to them in their memories.

It's a beautiful experience—a gift of love—when a child obeys to please us. It should make us both very happy.

How can you be sure that a rule is "good"?   *Your answer:*

1. *Is the rule well-defined?* If it is open to doubts as to the time it's to be accomplished, the exact way it's to be accomplished or the number of times it is to be done, then it's not a good rule. We need to consider if it is possible for a child of this age with his limitations (he is not an adult) to accomplish the rule regularly. A rule that requires extraordinary attention and effort—anything unusual—is not fair or just.

2. *Is it enforceable?* Do we have the capability of remembering the rule and following through on it ourselves? Are we going to be around when the rule fits in order to be able to enforce it?

3. *Is it understandable and is it understood?* Are we willing to take the time and effort to explain it? In other words, most rules need more than an announcement. They have to be explained. They have to be defined, along with the reasons behind them, in order to be digested by our children.

4. *Does it express the value we want it to?* Is it consistent with the other values we have—or want to have? Spelling out our value puts the compliance to the rule on a meaningful level. All too often, because something suddenly upsets us or causes us worry or

concern, we quick make up a rule. But what is its purpose? It should be to help the child understand what is expected of him. By doing what he is supposed to, the child takes into his life some of the value that is important to us. If a specific rule does not accomplish that, we should either omit the rule or change it.

5. *Is it supported by both of us?* Obviously, any rule that is not agreed upon by both of us is wrong. If it means something to only one parent—even if the other goes along with the rule because he has no particular objection to it, the children will sense the unevenness. We need to talk it out between us, and then talk it over with the children. It takes a long time to get a rule defined and passed.

6. *Will it build family relationships?* That's the highest purpose of a rule. If we make one because all the other parents in the neighborhood have it, or because we've heard a lecture by a child psychologist or read an article in a magazine and it seemed reasonable, it still may not work in our family. Maybe it's a rule we grew up with or our parents expect us to have with our kids. No matter what the pressure, we should put in only the ones we believe are best and proper for *our* family relationships.

7. *Is it positive rather than negative?* If most of our rules are don'ts, then there's something wrong. The whole orientation is out of whack. We need a lot of *do's*. Do's give people constructive action.

8. *Does it foster the well-being of all of us?* A rule with a "gotcha" mentality behind it—one that is aimed at catching the child—is expecting failure. Or, if a rule is aimed at only one member of the family, then it's not a good one.

A rule that is for the well-being of all of us will become a credit to each member of the family. It will lead us to a deeper appreciation of one another. It will be life-giving!

Enjoy! Enjoy! Enjoy!

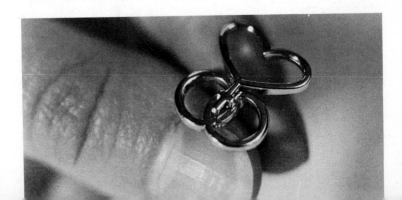